Julia Parker dedicated the past decade to learning about and working with the elderly and their loved ones. She supports and teaches elders, their families, and health care workers to understand the impacts of aging, dementia, and the health care system. Julia continues to work as a registered nurse certified in gerontology, an educator, speaker, writer, and consultant. Julia lives with her family in Idaho where she leads an active lifestyle and pursues her many passions.

To my family in gratitude for all their love and support
over the years.

Julia Parker

NAVIGATING ELDER CARE

AUSTIN MACAULEY PUBLISHERS™

LONDON • CAMBRIDGE • NEW YORK • SHARJAH

Ordering Information
Quantity sales: Special discounts are available on quantity purchases by corporations, associations, and others. For details, contact the publisher at the address below.

Publisher's Cataloging-in-Publication data
Parker, Julia
Navigating Elder Care

ISBN 9781647504014 (Paperback)
ISBN 9781649790521 (Hardback)

Library of Congress Control Number: 2021908322

www.austinmacauley.com/us

First Published (2021)
Austin Macauley Publishers LLC
40 Wall Street, 33rd Floor, Suite 3302
New York, NY 10005
USA

mail-usa@austinmacauley.com
+1 (646) 5125767

Navigating Elder Care was made possible through the hundreds of conversations I shared with elders, their loved ones, and my colleagues in long-term care, dementia support, home health, and hospice as well as formal and informal support groups for families dealing with Alzheimer's and dementia. Much of what I learned over the past decade has been a mixture of research, education, and trial and error. I want to give a special thank you to everyone who believed in me even when my attempts failed at first.

Thank you to Austin Macauley for supporting me and working through the many drafts with me.

Let me start by saying that working with elders and their families has enriched my life in so many ways. This work has made me a kinder, more compassionate, more intentional person. I have gained so much from working with our aging population, and I want to give back to all those elders and their families by writing about all we have learned together through tears and laughter, through traumatic moments and peaceful endings, through frustration and success. This book is based on the hundreds of conversations I have had working as an elder care nurse. I share it with you so that your journey might be easier.

I grew into my passion for elder care nursing. When I was in nursing school starting my second career, I thought I wanted to do all kinds of other types of nursing – birth, babies, emergency rooms, cardiac care – but not elder care. Some nurses have these wonderful stories about caring for their grandparents, volunteering in nursing homes as a child, and always wanting to be an elder care nurse. As much as I loved and looked up to my grandfather, and wanted to do whatever I could for him, he was independent until the last few weeks of his life and he took care of us more than we took care of him. I stumbled into working in geriatrics. The nursing shortage in the United States means that we are constantly recruited to work in other positions.

I was recruited into a job working in elder care. I decided to give it a try. Although I stumbled into elder care nursing, I totally I fell in love with it. The first resident that sparked my passion for elder care was Darlene.

Darlene had just lost her husband who had apparently been doing a lot to manage Darlene and her Alzheimer's disease at home before he died from lung cancer. I had recently gotten some training on dementia care through the National Council of Certified Dementia Practitioners[i], and I practiced my new skills on Darlene. After dealing with some challenges like peeing in the trash can, and insisting she hadn't eaten right after I had just seen her eat, I started using my new-found skills working with someone with dementia. I scheduled reminders to go to the toilet and showed her over and over where it was in her room. We put a big picture of a toilet on the bathroom door, and eventually, she knew where the toilet was and stopped peeing in the trash can. I learned not to take her plate away when she finished a meal so that she had the cue that she had just eaten what was on the plate. We also fed her more because she had lost so much weight at home while living with her ailing husband. I helped her through a hospital visit after a broken hip when the hospital couldn't keep her calm and in bed, and eventually, I helped her family engage hospice care so that she could live her last days in comfort. I stumbled through and found my way to helping Darlene and her family. But the best part was that when I figured things out, I brought Darlene moments of happiness and contentment, and as I got to know her, her preferences and became a safe resource for her, we had moments of joy, and I loved that as much as she did.

As I learned to work effectively as an elder care nurse, I loved the depth of getting to know elders and their families over time. I love the holistic approach of senior care, because it emphasizes many areas of life including physical, spiritual, cognitive, social, and medical care. I got to know my elderly clients, and I often became an advocate for them, and a part of their lives. I saw how people lived and died well. I learned the problems that arose to make both life and death more difficult. I learned so much from my experiences with elders and their families, and all the systems they navigate to make the best of their later years. I found myself answering the same questions and working through the same difficulties over and over for seniors and their families and friends. After a few years and a little more training, I wanted to share my growing knowledge and expertise with people. I ran a support group for the Alzheimer's Association, and I helped my friends and community members when I could. I loved helping people navigate the complexities of elder care. But there weren't always enough hours in the day to help everyone that I wanted to. That's when I decided to start writing down as much as I could to help anyone with the time and inclination to learn about helping elders manage their later years when they might need help. This book is a reflection of the years of education, hands-on experience, and problem-solving I did over my time as an elder care nurse – a job that I still do almost every day. Often I think of navigating care for elders in need in terms of an experience I once had while traveling in Costa Rica. An experience that left me turned upside-down and gasping until I got myself turned around. When helping seniors, problems can creep up on you, and then they can keep coming and knock you around a bit.

You have to face the waves, because they are coming in and they are unpredictable. I learned this the hard way. Standing in shallow water on the beach in Costa Rica. I was facing the beach so I could keep an eye on my young daughter playing in the sand with others. I felt the calm rhythm of the waves on my legs until suddenly, it wasn't calm anymore. I got slammed under the water and turned over and over, coming up gasping for air. As soon as I caught my breath, another wave came and down I went again, trying to roll with it and holding my breath. When I came up sputtering, I knew I couldn't keep my back to the ocean. Now I know this is the perfect metaphor for the unpredictability of elder care. Sometimes the waves are gentle and manageable, but sometimes they leave you tumbling and gasping for air. It's best to know what is coming.

The waves of senior care are relentless – big or small, fast or slow, gentle or crashing. This book will help you face the waves and manage the multitude of possible responses. I will try here to provide insights, resources, and assistance to make the navigation easier. From many years of working in senior care, I am here to tell you that you are not alone and that although families and people are unique, I have seen many combinations of difficulties, and have helped people successfully handle them. Sometimes I do say that I have seen it all in elder care, but usually someone makes a liar of me the next day if I do say that. This week one of my patients, a former elementary school teacher, became delusional because of an infection on top of her dementia, and she spent an hour in her apartment talking to a class of school children who were not actually there. The month before, a patient admitted to Hospice went eleven days without food or fluids before she passed away. A few weeks before that a patient walked down the stairs of her assisted living dragging her wheelchair behind her, because she could not find the elevator. So, I will say I have seen almost everything in senior care, but there is always a new phenomenon, joy or difficulty to face. I hope the scenarios and tools I discuss in this book will help you manage whatever aging brings.

This book is written for helpers – adult sons and daughters, loved ones, spouses, friends, and neighbors who have taken on the responsibility to help someone else through the later years of life. The people who help elders who cannot manage the complexities of living on their own. This does not mean that I think all elders cannot manage life for themselves. I recognize that many of them can. Although this book is written with the helper audience in mind, others who want to better navigate senior care can benefit from it. So, if you are anticipating navigating senior care for yourself, or if you are working in senior care and support, this book can also be for you.

I want to start with a thank you note. First, I just want to acknowledge the work you are doing to be a caregiver and supporter, and the fact that you have picked up a book on navigating elder care means that you are really trying to do this well. You are showing so much love and compassion. So, if no one else is thanking you, let me say thank you. Thank you for caring. Thank you for spending the time. Thank you for making an effort. Thank you for the love and support you are giving another human in need. This can be a difficult time both for seniors and for their families and friends. For adults, not being able to totally take care of yourself is a very difficult time in our independently-minded culture. Being dependent on others can hurt your pride, and it can be scary. This stress and fear means that seniors aren't always at their best with their loved ones who are trying to help. They can take those frustrations out on people they love and people who care for them. So, I want to say thank you for helping.

I know that lots of people have opinions about how you are caring for your loved one. People seem to love to share unsolicited opinions about three things in life: child birth, diets and elder care. Who knows why they feel the need to share that with others. "I would never put MY mother in a nursing home." "You need to get your uncle to drink celery juice to cure his Alzheimer's." Whatever the unsolicited judgment or advice you might get, please know that there are as many ways to help elders as there are elders. Short of abuse and neglect, there really is not a right or wrong way to manage and provide care. I hope my insights help you make the best decisions for you. Whether you want to provide all the care at home yourself, or you want to find a safe place for a senior, you just do the best you can. No one really knows the right decisions for your life. So, let me say again, thank you for helping. It means a lot for older people to have an advocate, and you are doing that for someone else.

As a gerontology nurse with experience in dementia care, senior living, and nursing homes, I help others work through dilemmas in aging and senior care every day. If I am not helping someone at work, I am talking with friends and neighbors throughout my community who are struggling with the many aspects of elders in need of support. Currently, I am blessed with healthy, independent parents, so for now, I can maintain a more clinical view of this world. Sometimes, it helps to have a professional perspective. When my time comes, I am sure I will still experience the same struggles as everyone else. However, what I have and what I am offering in this book, is many years of experience, study and work in gerontology and elder care.

Does this daughter sound like you?

So, this is my life now. I visit Mom on Sundays, but I also buy her snacks, water bottles, and incontinence supplies. I make sure Meals-on-Wheels delivers to her house twice a week. I take her to doctor's appointments, nag her about using her walker, encourage her to eat, hire help that she hates, read up on her medications, and worry about her going out on the back patio where the concrete is uneven. And now, when I thought I might have this figured out, she fell. She didn't tell me she fell. I discovered that after telling the cleaners I hired not to do her laundry, she fell while carrying her clothes basket. I found out because she was covered with bruises on her right arm and hip. I saw the bruises on her arm, then she confessed to falling, and showed me the damage to her hip. We were lucky. She could get up on her own, and she didn't break any bones. She says she doesn't want to move into one of those "old folks" homes and she insists she doesn't need help. Clearly, she needs something. But is leaving home and losing some freedom worth keeping her safe? I just don't know.

Do these long-time friends and neighbors sound like you?

I take a meal over to Fran twice a week. My husband mows her lawn, and we have shoveled her walk for years. She has seemed content with her life. Fran is careful, but she is slow to get around. She drives herself to the grocery, doctor's office and bank, and goes to the senior center once or twice a week for meals. Lately though, we found out that she gave money to someone who called collecting for charity. We think it might be a scam. And she said that we stole her car keys, and she didn't drive for a week. We found the keys for her in her dresser drawer, but she still insists that "someone" stole them, and then put them back. I noticed some new medications on her counter for her blood pressure, but it doesn't look like she was taking them. We put them in those daily boxes for her, and when I check I see that sometimes she takes them and sometimes she doesn't. We want her to be safe, and we are happy to help, but we aren't sure how much more we can or should do.

Does this son sound like you?

My dad needs me. He has Alzheimer's and maybe some other dementia from lifelong alcohol abuse. After his third wife died, I was all he had left. So we moved him from Wisconsin to Washington to be near us. The thing is, I don't even really know him. He left us when I was in pre-school.

I talked to him a few times a year, and a few years I went out to spend a couple of weeks with him in the summer; needless to say, we weren't close. Now, the assisted living facility is calling me all the time – "your dad needs this," "your dad needs that," "your dad is sick." I visit most weeks. I take him to the doctor's appointments. But I don't know how much I really want to do. Now, I have to make decisions about his medical treatment and end-of-life possibilities, and on top of that he is running out of money. It's too much.

There are so many different scenarios. And hopefully there are many happy scenarios too – families who are close, elders who makes their wishes known, and elders who really don't need much help. There are as many variations as there are people in the world. I wrote this book to lend a helping hand to people in many kinds of situations helping elders navigate care.

This book is divided into the following sections:

1. How to define needs.
2. The effects of aging that commonly occur in an elder's life and healthcare.
3. Navigating the many types and levels of outside care an elder may need.
4. Healthy ways of coping with the ups and downs of helping elders.

In each of these sections, I will bring in voices of helpers and professionals to try to shape the conversation with real stories. I will also provide tips, conversation guides, and outside resources for you. You can also use my website: www.juliaparkerconsulting.com to download forms from this book.

How to Define Needs

Life is made of a series of events, emotions, attachments and, yes, needs. We are going to focus on these needs as they pertain to aging and care. In order to clearly delineate needs and meet those needs, we can break them down into a serios of tasks that have to be done. It is as if you broke down your day into the ultimate to-do list.

To-Do

- Get out of bed
- Use the toilet
- Make coffee and toast
- Eat
- Wash dishes
- Put on glasses
- Get out your vitamins
- Take vitamin
- Brush teeth
- Pay bills
- Drive to the post office
- Mail bills
- Go to the grocery

- Pick out food
- Drive home
- Put food away
- Take a nap!

I hate to boil down lives into types of tasks we need to get done. We all know there is more to navigating eldercare than that. However, for the purposes of this section, daily life will be broken down into complex tasks and personal tasks. Difficulties with mobility, dexterity, and cognition lead to problems completing our daily tasks. In healthcare, these tasks are called "Activities of Daily Living" often abbreviated to "ADLs." These may not be the things that make up the joys of life (ability to give a good hug is not an ADL), but they do serve as benchmarks for how well a person can care for him or herself in the world.

Complex tasks (also called Independent Activities of Daily Living in the healthcare field) reflect how well someone can manage life in interaction with different aspects of a community such as banks, grocery stores, or transportation systems.

So, in the list of tasks above, ADL or personal tasks would include:

- Get out of bed
- Use the toilet
- Eat
- Take your vitamin
- Put on glasses
- Brush teeth

- Take a nap.

And IADL or complex tasks would include:

- Make coffee and toast
- Remember your vitamin
- Pay bills
- Drive to post office
- Mail bills
- Go to the grocery
- Pick out food
- Drive home
- Put food away.

Below, I provide a more general table of personal and complex tasks based on the Center for Medicare and Medicaid guidelines[ii]. Most of these lists come from federal definitions so that reimbursement can be provided for some types of care.

Category of IADL/ Complex Task	Description
Manage finances	Paying bills, writing checks or using electronic transfers or bank cards, knowing a bank account balance, watching for fraud
Transportation	Driving his/her own car, using public transit or managing other transportations services such as buses, cabs or Ubers.
Shopping	Getting to a store and buying adequate and appropriate items or accomplish this remotely via internet or phone.
Preparing meals	Cooking, heating up meals or ordering food.
Communication	Using phone/communication devices – the ability to use a phone (even if it is just a landline!)
Medication management	Knowing which medications to take, when and why, and remembering to take them.
Housework	Keeping a home clean enough to be safe and healthy.

Table 1: Understanding Complex Tasks or IADLs

Difficulty with complex tasks may require finding assistance while a senior can still stay at home. This might require family to step in and assist, but it does not require care in a senior living facility. Friends, families, and community programs can help with these complex tasks. Consider dividing tasks among various family members or helpers for an elder. For example, if there are three siblings, one son could help prepare and freeze meals and stock the kitchen with snacks, one son may set up a medication management system whether that is basic or a sophisticated computerized system that provides alerts to him if medications aren't taken or he can just stop by once a day to help in person, and a third son may commit to transporting to and attending medical appointments. If these aren't enough or people aren't available hired in-home, caregivers can manage most of these tasks.

Personal Tasks or Activities of Daily Living

Day-to-day tasks are broken into complex tasks (IADLs) and personal tasks (ADLs). Personal tasks are those that provide care for your own body such as showering or brushing your hair. A complete list of ADLs as defined by the Center for Medicare and Medicaid is in the table below.

Category of ADL/Personal Task	Description
Feeding	The ability to get food from plate to mouth. (This does not include food preparation or cooking.)
Toileting	The ability to know when to use the toilet, urinate or defecate, clean the perineum and change incontinence products when needed.
Grooming	Brushing hair and teeth, cleaning dentures, shaving, applying lotion or make-up if desired.
Bathing	Safely showering, bathing or giving a sponge bath, shampooing hair.
Dressing	Putting on and taking off clothes, including socks and shoes.
Walking (ambulating)	Being able to move around with or without an assistive device. This means that a person who can move him/herself in a wheelchair can "ambulate."
Transferring	Moving from one place to another such as from the bed to standing, from bed to wheel chair, from toilet to standing etc.

Table 2: Understanding Personal Tasks or ADLs

To put it simply, personal tasks simply involve someone else touching your body. Losing these skills is very upsetting for most people. It makes them feel vulnerable and dependent whether they are relying on a family member or a professional caregiver. Although there is the occasional person who really doesn't seem to mind. I have had a few patients who walk around naked or use the toilet while carrying on a full conversation with nurses or caregivers, but they are the exception. Difficulty accepting care is common and creates a barrier to staying healthy and clean. Refusing assistance especially in the bath or shower can cause a lot of strife between seniors, caregivers, and families. Professional care staff should document any refusals of care, and if it is a consistent problem, they should notify the family that there is a problem. This can be an especially big problem in a caregiver is of the opposite sex. Many older women especially prefer a female caregiver. This can usually be arranged by professional in-home care agencies or residential care facilities. Because more women work in the field than men, it can be more difficult to pair male clients with male caregivers if that is needed. Another, aspect of the difficulty with refusing personal care is that seniors have a right to refuse. No one can force them to accept care even if they need it. Of course, we want elders to be able to direct their own care, but this can create issues with hygiene. So, these struggles can pit the rights of the elder against what might be in their best interest. The challenges of refusing help can be approached in a variety of well-practiced methods. Some tried and true practices are listed in the table below. You can also be creative and think of ways to individualize care and make personal care more successful.

Strategy	Examples
Learning the elder's preferences	Showers in the evening or morning. Favorite soaps or shampoos. Baths or showers.
Adjusting the environment	Keep bathroom warm. Provide warm soft towels. Provide robe for modesty and comfort. Use a shower chair for comfort. Allow resident to start shower partially clothed. Make bathroom and shower look inviting and not like a high school locker room – especially in care facilities.
Changing the approach	Discuss shower ahead of time. Make declarative statements: "Time for your shower!" works better than "Would you like to take a shower now?" Encourage as much independence as is safe. Provide as much privacy as possible – close the door, close the shower curtain Re-approach later if you get a "no"

	Try a different caregiver or family member.
Adjust your expectations	If all else fails clean as much as possible. Let the senior wash his or her face, hands and whatever else they can reach. (Almost everyone can reach their own private parts.) Use a built in bidet or "smart toilet" for cleaning perineum. Provide disposable wipes for armpits and genitals for more frequent use.

Table 3: Approaches to Reduce Refusals of Bathing

Providing Personal Care

Many seniors want to stay home as long as possible and not move to residential care. According to an annual survey by LeadingAge three-quarters or more of older adults report a desire to stay in their homes. In 2019, older baby boomers did report less leaning toward in-home care if they needed daily help. In other words, as we reach the baby boomer generation there seems to be more acceptance of residential care. [iii] Another concern of older adults is the fear of becoming a burden to their families. It's no surprise that people have mixed feelings about how to best get care for themselves or their loved ones. I have seen residents who thrive in an assisted living or memory care setting, and others who never stop wanting to go home. It's important to keep an open mind about care when you start to approach in-home care and other options. Hybrid models in which family, hired caregivers and sometimes residential care will help balance a lot of issues. Providing personal care for others can be done at home. However, it is physically and emotionally hard on the caregiver to do this for a full day every day, so these tasks should be shared among several people. Adults that need physical assistance are heavy and can cause injuries to others especially back injuries and falls. Personal care is especially difficult if both the elder and the caregiver have limited abilities such as if this is a married couple relatively close in age. There are many options to getting help with personal care. Assistance can be divided up in blocks of times or by tasks. Assistance can be shared among family members, and other close friends. Hiring caregivers to come into the home for at least part of each day can also be helpful. A friend confided in me recently that her father wants her to quit her job and move to another state to take care of her mother. He told her that is the way it was done in the past and that is what he expects from her. Both parents are in their late 90s and have been independent until very recently. Now her mother needs help and it is wearing out her father. But she has a life in another state – friends, a husband, a job, and a small business. She also knows that even if she does move there to help her parents, she won't be able to do it alone. Families that are scattered across the country with all adults working in their respective places make it very difficult to go back to the old model of caring for parents in their home. In addition, as medical care has improved, elders live much longer while needing care. Making this more than a few months' commitment. Some families manage this, but they are very rare.

So, instead of full-time family in-home care, we start to look at hybrid models of care. After family in-home care, the next step is usually hiring a professional (paid) caregiver. In most states, anyone can call themselves a caregiver. There is not a professional credential or license to work in someone else's home to provide care. This means that families need to carefully vet any potential in-home worker. It is so tempting to hire someone from your community instead of going through an agency, because agencies are expensive. You may want to pay someone $15 per hour to work in your loved one's home and not pay any overhead or insurance, and agencies are currently $25-32 per hour. Please be cautious hiring a caregiver without an agency. It may not be worth the savings. Caregivers need to be trained and experienced so they do not hurt themselves or your loved one. Hiring through a reputable agency means that caregivers have been trained, and they have had a criminal and license background check. Also, they have oversight from a licensed agency. In addition, relying on one person that has been hired with no back up means that anytime they are sick or can't come to work, you have to scramble to fill in. An agency will provide a substitute caregiver when needed. Not all agency caregivers are perfect and if you have any problems, communicate quickly with the agency, but my experience is that there are many more problems with non-licensed or independent caregivers. If you do hire someone independently, make sure a trusted friend or family member is monitoring the situation. Stop in daily and at different times to see how things are going, and set expectations regarding what you want the caregiver to do. Having someone sit in the living room looking at their phone for hours is not worth your money. Listen to your elderly loved one's opinion, have different people stop in to check how things are going. Use cameras if you must, but make sure the caregiver and your loved one is aware. Just take creative measures to make sure you are paying attention to what is happening.

Seniors and families can get very attached to in-home caregivers and this sometimes means that they let their expectations and standards for care slide. Remember that it is the caregiver's job to help the senior at home and not vice versa. I do believe in taking care of employees, paying them well and providing good working conditions, but I have witnessed many cases in which an elder is taking care of their caregiver and may be taken advantage of. This often revolves around finances. Caregiving is a fairly low paying job and sometimes caregivers struggle, but it gets very complicated if a client starts supporting that caregiver through gifts, groceries or loans. If you are concerned about the financial well-being of a caregiver, see if you can afford to increase his/her salary in a formal way instead of creating a default system of requests and indulgences.

Common Problems Associated with the Aging Body

Now that we have covered how to discuss needs, we are going to have a brief overview of how aging commonly affects the body and its ability to perform daily tasks.

Mobility

Musculoskeletal changes, disease, and inactivity decreases mobility as we age. The freedom to move as you want, when you want, is a luxury that most of us have for only parts of our lives. While we may group people into able-bodied and disabled, this concept is better considered as gradations of ability. A few years ago, I heard the concept of "temporarily able." This really struck me considering that during our lifetimes, we will go through periods of different abilities. As babies, we were unable to walk, as toddlers we had unsteady gaits and had trouble feeding ourselves, at later periods in our lives we may have had changes in mobility from a broken ankle or some other illness or injury, and as we reach our elder years, we may again have disabilities. People who are temporarily able whether that is due to being young, being lucky or getting lots of medical help tend to forget to recognize what they have until it is gone. Most of us know the frustration of having to use crutches or having a broken arm. These periods of disability will hopefully open our eyes to the struggles of others with mobility problems.

As we age, we commonly have declines in balance, muscle strength, flexibility, joint mobility, and endurance. These declines have the effect of making it less comfortable and more frightening to keep moving. People know that falls are a common problem for the elderly that these falls can have dire consequences due to the risk of fractures. So, when the natural declines of aging start, seniors may feel like they cannot safely continue to exercise creating a downward spiral of deconditioning and immobility. Not moving is the worst thing we can do as we age.

Continuing to move is the most important intervention in declining mobility. Finding any type of activity is helpful. I have encountered so many seniors that are on this downward spiral, I'm not even sure where to start with examples. Recently, I was working at a senior living community that had four buildings. All were connected by indoor passageways. Meals were served in one building next to the most independent housing building. Yet the hottest item in the place was an electric scooter. Everyone had them, whether they needed them or not, so that they could zip around from one building to another. Not only did they have the ability to walk, they were all retired and had the time too. In another situation, I talked with a lady in her early 70s who was still hiking, but when she went to the airport she got them to take her in a wheelchair to the gate just because they never questioned her. It was like a perk of aging that she felt she deserved. There was no reason for it. Now that we have experienced months of COVID-19 restrictions in 2020, seniors are finding that their strength and mobility is greatly reduced by spending much, if not all, of their time withing their houses, apartments or rooms in residential care. Eliminating even a bi-weekly walk around the grocery store, or a visit to a neighbor's home is causing decreases in activity that need to be compensated for with more regular and deliberate exercise. The consequence of this is increased falls in residential facilities and decreased ability for self-care overall. Elders, just like the rest of us, need to move as much as we can. Use it or lose it!

Mobility Devices and Helpers

One way to improve mobility is to use some of the many assistive devices as an intermediary to gain strength safely or as permanent support. If you are helping an elder, I implore you to help your loved one find and develop the ability to use devices to improve mobility. We all know the adage of "use it or lose it." Inactivity is biggest threat to mobility. So whatever training and investment needed to adapt to new devices is worth the time and expense. Using a wheelchair is better than staying in bed. Using a walker is better than being in a wheelchair. A cane, a brace, railings or grab bars in the bathroom – anything that increases mobility will help. Elders can often get assistance from occupational therapists or physical therapists in their own homes or residential care facility to find the best and safest devices. Occupational therapists and physical therapists can help teach and develop best practices for using assistive devices. Occupational therapists help people use their equipment and environment in optimal ways. Physical therapists help people improve their bodies to increase mobility, balance, and functional strength.

Adapted exercise programs for the elderly can help people continue to use their muscles in a safe way. If a senior has increasing mobility problems, many local recreation departments have classes like "sit and be fit," weight lifting or senior yoga that can fit anyone's ability. Specialized programs to help with mobility for the unique challenges of Parkinson's disease are especially promising. These classes include boxing to fight Parkinson's disease and specialized dance classes. Music and dance can really help people smooth out movements and stay motivated to keep going.

Even the most frail or most compromised person can benefit from movement and exercise. Although, sometimes we joke that we want to wrap someone in bubble wrap and keep them still so they don't get hurt, that would be the worst idea for them. Mobility is the enemy of frailty. So encourage movement in any way you can.

Now that I have been on my soap box about moving and mobility, I can add that a walker, a wheel chair or an even a power scooter increases mobility but mobility can also be enhanced by vision correction, adaptation and remodeling to homes or public places, changes in bathrooms and devices that help with hand mobility reach and grip. Thankfully, there are many options to help adapt to mobility problems. It's important to get the help of a therapist, experienced nurse, or even a senior care support group to think through the many options.

Walkers and Canes

Because maintaining mobility is one of the most important parts of healthy aging, I want to detail some of the pros and cons of different approaches. There are a variety of common mobility devices that can help maintain balance and assist where strength is needed. Canes can help if someone has a weakness in one leg that is predictable or pain in one leg that can be alleviated by taking some weight off one side. However, canes are not commonly employed anymore because canes tend to also get tangled up with feet and legs, and they are frequently dropped increasing fall risk. Walkers now come in a variety of shapes, sizes, colors and costs. The best fit and particular features can be ordered by physical therapists. Although, anyone can buy a walker from an internet retailer, there are specific features that help with different issues. Some walkers accommodate small frames and some are designed for taller or heavier people. Walkers with just two wheels help the most with stability and are easier controlled. Walkers with four wheels are a convenience, but the user has to be able to slow down on his own, and use brakes with his hands. Specialized walkers are made for people with Parkinson's disease that counter the jerky movements and hesitation associated with this disease. A safety note about 4-wheel walkers: I know that many people use the seat of their fancy 4-wheel walkers like a wheel chair either pedaling themselves backwards of having someone push them while on the walker seat. Just… please don't. The small wheels and high center of gravity make this dangerous for the rider. The seats on 4-wheel walkers are made for resting, not riding.

Walkers also need to be checked and maintained for safety and to maintain their best performance. Brakes can wear out and they are very important for stability if they are used to assist people to stand up out of a chair or if people use the seat feature. Wheels should be checked and maintained for smooth walking. And the seat, handles, and stability of the legs of the walkers should also be checked and tightened frequently.

Wheelchairs

Wheelchairs may be necessary if a senior does not have enough strength or stability for walking with a walker, or they can be helpful for long distances when a walk is too tiring. As with walkers, there are different types of wheelchairs. Transport wheelchairs are lighter weight, and can be used if you want to help someone go where they would not normally have the stamina to go like to a grandchild's graduation or for a trip around the local park. Transport chairs are easier to fold and put into the trunk or backseat of a car. These types of wheelchairs are great if you know your loved one might be limited by fatigue, but doesn't need a wheelchair frequently. In addition, they are less expensive than a standard wheelchair.

If an elder needs a wheelchair most of the time, transport wheelchairs don't provide enough cushioning, and this can cause pain and even pressure sores. Transport chairs are also less durable. A wheelchair for everyday use has more padding and are sturdier. Even when wheelchairs are used, people can and should be encouraged to continue to try to keep as much strength as they can for moving in and out of the wheelchair, standing and/or walking even for a short time, and even pedaling on the floor to move themselves improves endurance and maintains more independence. A physical therapist or a reputable wheelchair company can provide suggestions for fitting wheelchairs. There are differences for height, weight, stability and abilities. Specialized reclining chairs can be helpful if an elder has trouble keeping his/her body straight and holding up his/her head if needed. Explore these different sizes, and configurations because it is important to get the right version. Further, wheelchairs can be expensive and they do wear out. If you get a doctor's order, health care plans, including Medicare, may pay for an appropriate wheelchair, and can replace it every five years.

Wheelchairs should be maintained by a medical supply company. Brakes should always hold firmly. Edges should be smooth to prevent scratches and skin tears. Attachable footrests should always be available and used when anyone else is pushing the chair. If footrests are not used an elder can get their foot and ankle caught and twisted under the chair causing injury.

Remodeling and Home Adaptations

Reconfiguring homes for mobility problems helps seniors thrive outside a residential care facility. Bathrooms seem to create the biggest risk for falls, and a few simple redesigns can alleviate many problems. Even if people are not using a wheelchair or other mobility devices, design changes can improve safety and mobility:

- A taller commode, or a sturdy seat riser
- Grab bars on the walls around the toilet
- Grab bars in the shower
- A shower bench
- A walk in shower

Toilets are low! I had some experience with this recently after running my first trail half-marathon. My quadriceps were sore and weak for days after, and to be honest the toilet provided the biggest challenge. I really struggled to sit in any kind of controlled way and then had to lean far forward to get back up. I was a fall waiting to happen. I knew in theory that toilets were often too low for people with limited mobility, but boy did that experience drive that home for me! You don't have to run a half-marathon yourself to learn this, you could just take my word for it! A taller toilet is the safest, cleanest replacement for those low toilets. These can be purchased and installed by plumbers or if you are handy can be purchased at a home supply store. You can buy other devices that sit on top of the seat, but they are often unstable and they are difficult to keep clean. A bedside commode is designed to be used when a person (such as a patient in the hospital) cannot safely walk to the bathroom. These look a bit like a lawn chair with a removal bucket underneath and can also be used over a toilet (take the bucket out) to provide a higher seat and arm rests. Again though, these are less stable and can be difficult to clean.

Standing or sitting in a shower is easier for most older people than getting in and out of a bathtub. A shower with a low or no step is ideal although you will have to take some time and effort configuring the shower head to make sure the bathroom floor isn't covered in water after a shower. Flexible plastic strips can be put in place for no step showers so that even someone in a wheelchair can roll in and then the water has a small barrier to keep it from running onto the floor. A completely wheelchair bound person can get a rolling bath chair made of plastic and mesh that can go into the shower too. Not many people need these at home, because many can transfer from a wheelchair to a shower bench for bathing with help.

There are many advertisements on television for walk in bathtubs for people with limited mobility who still enjoy a bath. Some people do really like them and find the whirlpool bath relaxing. But take extra time to check them out before making that financial commitment. The thing about walk in tubs is that people still need the strength to get themselves upright if they slip under the water. In addition, to use these, you have to get into the tub (naked) and then sit there while it fills up. In my experience, this is a long, cold wait for people who want a bath and it deters many people from using them very frequently. If you have already purchased a walk-in tub and are having this problem, you can wrap up in warm towels and toss them over the side as the water rises, but it is a discomfort for some people. And most still require some level of step up. It is less than getting in and out of a bathtub, but it is a step.

Another major area in making a home more mobility-friendly is to look at flooring and stairs. Decreasing the need to manage stairs can greatly improve mobility at home. That might mean reconfiguring a home to create a bedroom space on the main floor or building outdoor ramps to eliminate stairs coming in and out of the house. Cheaper fixes include making sure thresholds are flat and eliminating scatter rugs. Scatter rugs are notoriously dangerous for people prone to falls because they wrinkle and slip. Items traditionally housed in the basement like washers and dryers can also be changed to the main floor. Reconfiguring and decluttering a household can go a long way towards decreasing fall risks. The trade-off of investing in changes to the home could be worth the cost in delaying moving to a senior care facility that will have all of these adaptations already in place. At this time nursing homes cost $9,000 to $12,000 per month. Assisted living is usually between $3,500 and $8,000 per month. So, spending money on home renovations, even if the senior eventually needs to move into a senior living facility can be well worth the costs.

Upper Body Mobility Aids

Managing decreased strength and mobility in the upper body is also important to maintaining independence. Improving reach with "grabbers" – those long handles with a hinge on the end can be helpful for out of reach places, and decrease the need to bend over and possibly lose balance. (And just an aside, a large pair of kitchen tongs works just as well and will last longer.) Another helpful aid for arthritic, weak or shaky hands is a simple piece of foam that slides over the handle of any small implement. These were designed for silverware, but can be used for toothbrushes, paint brushes, pens and pencils. Arthritis makes it hard to hold small handles and these padded additions can make it possible to do much more with less fatigue. You can buy this foam in long tubes and cut it to whatever length you need.

Cups with lids without small handles can help with ease of hydration and prevent spills. Using bowls instead of plates or using a plate with a lip can help shaky or arthritic hands scoop food instead of chasing it around and often off the edge of a plate.

Specialty adaptive silverware exists for shaking hands as well. These devices can be more expensive than the simple foam handle, but they move to self-level to keep the spoon or fork steady as the handshakes. They are definitely worth trying out especially if you can work with an occupational therapist to help learn how to use them.

Sometimes you just have to be creative. A few months ago, I helped a woman who had limited mobility after a stroke. Her feet kept slipping off her power chair foot plate, and because she had tiny feet, they slipped to the side and under her chair. She had badly hurt her ankle by running forward on her own foot. We had the power chair company representative come in to see if he could change the foot plate, but the company had no useful adaptations to offer. So I cut a pool noodle into two short lengths and then split one side. We slid these onto the sides of her foot plate. Voila! There was no more space for her feet to slip under her power chair. The pool noodle was even purple, her favorite color. Since we are talking about pool noodles, I will let you know that these versatile little pieces of foam can be used to pad sharp corners, and can be put under a fitted sheet to keep people with limited mobility from rolling out of bed.

I can't catalogue every piece of adaptive equipment, clothing, helpers and mobility devices here, but I encourage you to seek out products, and simple solutions that help. Sometimes it just takes a small adjustment like zippers instead of buttons or rearranging furniture for easier movement. Put your heads together with others helping your loved one and the seniors themselves to make simple and creative changes that improve mobility and independence.

We are going to move on from the general area of mobility and adaptations to common diseases and conditions and their effects of day-to-day life.

Common Health Problems and Diseases in the Elderly – A Lay Person's Guide

Over my years as an elder care nurse, I have become familiar with many common chronic illnesses that affect seniors. Although I cannot write a review of every ailment someone might have in their later years, I can give you a brief and understandable primer on common issues. This is not a medical book, but it is a translation in lay terms of the function and implications of common chronic diseases.

Much of a nurse's job is translating medical jargon into understandable and relevant information. Hopefully, this will provide a jumping off point for you to do more research on relevant issues for your loved one's situation.

Heart Failure

Heart failure also known as Congestive Heart Failure is the loss of muscle tone in the heart. Hearts can be damaged in a variety of ways or can simply start to wear out. As the heart loses muscle tone it becomes larger and "floppy." This makes the heart inefficient at moving blood through the body. At first the heart tries harder by increasing the number of beats per minute so heart rate increases and people tire more easily. In addition, an inefficient heart means that blood pressure is decreased and systems that require movement of blood (which is basically all of them) begin to fail. For example, as kidneys filter toxins from the blood they require a certain amount of pressure. If the pressure is too low, then fluid backs up in the blood vessels and leaks into tissue under the skin. This causes swelling known as edema, and this edema tends to be worst in the feet and legs because they are lower than the heart for most of the day. In worse cases, fluids might build up in other areas of the body including the lungs as they require a great deal of blood flow. So, with heart failure also comes fluid build-up in places like the feet, legs, under eyes and in the lungs. Fluid build-up can get bad enough that it affects the whole body (this is called anasarca). Two types of medications are often needed to treat for heart failure over the long term — medication to slow the heart rate, and medication to help eliminate excess water from the body. Beta blockers (Metoprolol, Toprol) are used to slow the heart rate. Diuretics (Lasix, Furosemide, HCTZ, Spironolactone) are used to eliminate excess water. These diuretics have the side effect of making people have to urinate a lot which often causes problems with sleep, incontinence and also result in a serious reluctance to stay on the medication – because no one wants to have to go to the bathroom every half hour. Swelling from edema can also create problems with skin due to the stretching and pressure leading to painful, tight skin, sores and open areas especially on the lower legs.

Hypertension

Hypertension or high blood pressure has a number of causes – some hereditary, some diet related. High blood pressure is related to narrowing and decreased flexibility of the blood vessels. The heart continues to try to pump the same amount of blood throughout the body, but the interior of the blood vessels become coated with plaque and the openings narrow. In addition, inflammation, plaque and pressure make the blood vessels less pliable. This means that the pressure from blood is higher in those smaller spaces. High blood pressure can further damage blood vessels especially small ones by the force on the walls of the vessels. This damages the kidneys, the brain and other systems, and also increases the risk of heart attacks and strokes.

Irregular Heart Rates

A normal heart rate is between 60 and 100 beats per minute. The heart beat also has a regular rhythm. The heart rhythm is simply the emptying of the four chambers of the heart. First, the upper chambers (atria) empty, and then the lower chambers (ventricles) of the heart empty. The heart is both a muscle, and an electrical conduction system. Changes in rhythm indicate underlying damage in the heart. The electrical system signals the muscles to contract in a regular rhythm, and allows the 4 chambers of the heart to fill and empty at the right times. If there is a problem in the electrical conduction of the message through the heart muscle, then the heart beats irregularly. An uncoordinated rhythm decreases the efficiency of the heart and can even get so bad that the heart cannot pump blood at all. Many people live with irregular heartbeats. One of the most common in the elderly is atrial fibrillation. In this condition, the top chambers of the heart are not getting the electrical signal and contract very rapidly (up to 300 times per minute), this makes it difficult for the heart to coordinate and blood pools in the lower chambers of the heart. When blood pools, it coagulates or clots. So, in atrial fibrillation, the greatest risk is that the patient can then develop a blood clot that makes its way out of the ventricle and gets stuck in a blood vessel – most commonly in the brain – causing a blockage to the blood in the brain also known as a stroke. For this reason, people with atrial fibrillation routinely take anti-coagulants (aka blood thinners) to prevent a clot.

Myocardial Infarctions (Heart Attacks)

The myocardium is the heart muscle. An infarct is dying muscle from a lack of blood and therefore oxygen supply. So, a myocardial infarction (MI) or in layperson's terms a heart attack, is damage to the heart muscle. A heart attack's effects can impact a small or large areas of the heart muscle. MI's damage the heart leading to the other two problems discussed earlier – an irregular heartbeat or heart failure. MIs have a very wide range of severity. The heart can just continue on without a lot of consequences from a small MI. Or, a heart can be so damaged from an MI as to be a life-ending event. MIs are usually the result of a gradual buildup of plaque from cholesterol or a blockage of a vessel from plaque or a blood clot blocking blood flow through one of the many vessels supplying oxygen-filled blood to the heart.

The signs of a heart attack vary widely. This makes it difficult for laypeople and even healthcare providers to identify a mild MI in progress unless they have access to laboratory results from chemicals in the blood or a heart monitor. As we know of all pain related symptoms, people experience pain very differently – some people are more sensitive and some people are more stoic. The Hollywood heart attack when a man (usually it's a man) clutches his chest and falls over is not very common. Heart attacks can be signaled by indigestion, pain or tingling in the left arm, pain in the left shoulder or jaw, and even a sense of "impending doom" or feeling that something just isn't right. I wish signals of a heart attack were easier to identify. In 15 years of nursing, I have never seen a classic, Hollywood style heart attack. I have had patients say that their back teeth hurt, that they feel like they hurt their shoulder but can't remember doing anything to it, patients complain of heartburn and feeling short of breath. One patient who fainted at some point then got himself back to his barn reported to the ER telling us that he thought a cow had kicked him in the chest. Anxiety and panic attacks can mimic a heart attack as well, and no one can really tell the difference without laboratory tests and/or an EKG (the test that shows a heart rhythm on a screen or strip of paper.) Lab tests are available in hospitals and EKGs can be done by an ambulance crew, in some doctor's offices or in the hospital. So, it's important to take any symptoms of an MI seriously and get qualified emergency help quickly.

Strokes/CVAs

What we commonly call a stroke in the US has the official name of a cerebral vascular accident (CVA). (Don't blame me, I don't name these things.) There are three types of cerebral vascular accidents or strokes: a hemorrhagic stroke, an ischemic stroke and a mini stroke (which also has the not so handy name of transient ischemic attack or TIA.) In a hemorrhagic stroke a blood vessel bursts in the brain. In an ischemic stroke, a blood vessel is blocked (usually by a blood clot) and the flow of blood is cut off to a certain part of the brain. A mini-stroke or TIA is a temporary blockage of blood flow to the brain. Hemorrhagic strokes are the most damaging, and require interventions to stop the bleeding such as emergency vascular surgery, IV medications to decrease blood pressure and reversing the effect of blood thinners if taken. Ischemic strokes can be treated with a strong blood thinner in the hospital or emergency room.

Dissolving the blood clot in the emergency room restores blood flow and limits the damage. Treatments available in hospitals are the reason time is so valuable if stroke symptoms occur. If an ischemic stroke can be caught early enough, a blood thinner can be used to dissolve the blood clot and return blood supply to the brain minimizing damage. The hemorrhagic stroke requires rapidly stopping the loss of blood into the brain tissue. A mini-stroke or TIA is also an ischemic stroke, but it dissipates within 24 hours without major medical intervention. The body manages to move the clot along or dissolve it, and symptoms clear within 24 hours. Damage to the brain is usually minimal, but multiple mini-strokes can result in problems over time. TIAs are a strong warning sign that another stroke can occur. Some people don't even realize they have had TIAs and the damage is seen with brain imaging. In my experience, there really is no way to tell the difference between a TIA and an ischemic stroke while they are happening. This is why we don't wait to get treatment. Even if your loved one has had previous TIAs and come out of them just fine, you don't know if this is a big stroke or a mini-stroke until it clears. So, if your loved one is still receiving treatment (meaning they are not on comfort care or in Hospice) then treat all stroke symptoms seriously.

Know the Signs of a Stroke

Facial droop on one side.

Drooping eyelid on one side.

Crooked smile.

Drooling.

Limp hand, arm or leg on one side.

Sudden inability to walk.

Uneven grip when you squeeze hands.

Slurred speech.

Suddenly inability to speak.

Confusion.

Head pain.

Loss of consciousness.

Arthritis and Joint Problems

Overtime, the vulnerable parts of our skeletons, the areas that move between bones – the joints – can wear down and have difficulty repairing themselves. The most common joint disease, osteoarthritis is present in many adults over 55. While associated with aging, it is not inevitable. Risk factors for osteoarthritis include obesity, muscle loss and injuries. This disease involves the wearing away of the joint's cushioning and increase in stiffness that results in painful and limited movements and sometimes constant aching.[iv]

In the elderly there are other fairly common reasons for joint pain. Gout, another type of joint pain results from a build-up of crystals in the joints. This build up causes swelling and heat in and around the joint. Gout can be treated when it flares up with medication, or medication such as allopurinol can be taken routinely to prevent flare ups. Gout can also be exacerbated by rich food and shell fish, so avoiding these can help decrease painful episodes. Rheumatoid arthritis can affect both young and old. It is an autoimmune disease that causes inflammation in the joints. This disease can also be treated symptomatically with medication when it flares up or it can be treated with medications to prevent flare ups. Medications for autoimmune diseases such as prednisone often come with a host of side effects and have to be carefully managed.

All types of joint pain can benefit from movement even though this might seem counterintuitive. A lack of movement just stiffens joints and makes flare ups worse and more common. Marie, my friend and physical therapist, tells me "motion is lotion" so keep moving those joints, and help decrease all kinds of arthritis pain. Heat and ice can also soothe aching joints and should be attempted for comfort. Heat helps relax surrounding muscles and ice reduces swelling associated with joint pain.

Kidney Failure

Damage to the kidneys is common as a result of two other common diseases in the elderly – hypertension and type II diabetes. Both of these diseases damage the small vessels in the kidneys that help filter waste from the blood. As these small vessels are damaged, kidney disease worsens. As kidneys fail to filter out enough toxins from the blood, symptoms such as nausea and confusion increase. Kidney disease requires correcting the causes of the disease such as lowering blood sugars and blood pressure. Kidney failure is usually a long process, but it can be acute (a fast onset) in cases where a patient is very sick or very dehydrated.

Type II Diabetes

I am literally writing this while eating tater tots, so no judgment… Type II diabetes is caused by excess ingestion of carbohydrates over time. It is true that some people are more prone to it than others and there may be some genetic link, but it is basically the wearing out of the pancreatic cells that produce insulin. Insulin is created in part of the pancreas, and it exists to help the body take carbohydrates eaten and turn them into energy for cells. When we eat an excess of carbohydrates (e.g. a plate of tater tots), the body doesn't need all of that so the energy is stored as fat. So, being overweight is a risk factor for diabetes. After a long time of pumping out lots of insulin the cells in the body start to ignore insulin. This is your body's way of saying "enough already" we are ignoring the insulin when it comes knocking to bring us carbohydrates that have become sugars. So, now the body has too much sugar just racing around in the blood stream and the cells are not answering the call of insulin. Thus, when a health care provider tests your blood sugar, it is too high. This happens over time, so people who see their doctor regularly get warnings over the years. At first, there are medications that help your body produce more insulin to overwhelm the cells and take the sugar for energy. If a person continued to eat too many carbohydrates then the pancreas eventually wears out and produces less insulin on its own. This is when people start taking insulin by injection. Injecting insulin while balancing carbohydrate intake and activities is difficult. This balance takes a lot of practice and is hard for many people to manage accurately.

High blood sugar as a result of diabetes damages the smallest blood vessels and this creates problems with vision, kidneys, nerve endings, cognition, and sexual function. In addition, just like sugary foods that mold faster than other foods, high sugar in the blood makes a great medium for growth of bacteria and yeasts, so people with high blood sugars are more susceptible to infections.

So many people in the US have Type II Diabetes, it is becoming normalized. But know that having high blood sugar has huge consequences for the body. So whatever you can do to lower it or to help your loved one lower it, do that. Outside of medication, know that losing weight, lowering carbohydrate and calorie intake, and exercise really help in lowering blood sugar. These actions also have no side effects like medication does. It's never too late to try to reduce the impacts of diabetes.

Bone Density

Why do older people fall and break a hip? Because bone density decreases with age making bones easier to break. So weakening femurs, vertebrae, ribs, collar bones, and arms break when they suffer the impact from a fall.

Decreased bone density is a life-long problem and it is not easy to improve bone density over time. Again, diet and exercise can help, but changes as older people provide a much smaller impact than being able to control something like blood sugar as with diabetes. There is controversy about medications used to improve bone density. They tend to have a pretty minimal impact on the problem and some are very expensive or have serious side effects. Your best efforts might be in helping prevent falls through the arrangement of the home, getting help with mobility and physical therapy or exercise classes designed to help. These classes might include senior yoga, Fit and Fall Proof,[v]

SAIL [vi] (Stay Active and Independent for Life), Silver Sneakers, or sit and be fit. These classes are specifically designed to safely perform movements needed for strength and balance to decrease fall risk. Classes to improve senior mobility can be found at many local senior centers, public recreation centers, on the internet and on public television.

Incontinence

One of the most common reasons that families move the elderly into residential care is to deal with incontinence. Incontinence is an embarrassing problem. It's smelly. It can leak outside of protection. Incontinence can limit an elder's socializations, activity and quality of life. There are a few reasons for incontinence: muscular, neurological and cognitive. The sphincters that control the bladder and bowels are muscles so losing muscle tone in the urethra coming from the bladder or in the rectum and anus cause leaking. People just don't have the strength to hold it in. This kind of leakage often occurs when pressure increases from sneezing, coughing or laughing. Neurological damage anyplace from the spine to the sphincters can make bladder or bowel elimination difficult. In the case of neurological damage, either someone can't go or they can't stop going. Cognitive changes may affect a person's ability to recognize the signs that they have to go to the toilet or they may forget where the bathroom is or how to use it.

There are a few ways to help deal with incontinence. Muscular incontinence can be helped with exercises such as pelvic floor (Kegel) exercises for both men and women. Medications exist to help with urinary urgency and frequency. These medications can be helpful, but also some are quite expensive and new research is indicating that they contribute to fall risk. Toileting programs such as reminders to go to the toilet frequently can be very successful for reducing accidents. Alarms can be set for every two hours as reminders while awake to keep the bladder from getting overly full. Schedules or reminders once or twice a day can help regulate and encourage bowel elimination. Scheduled toileting programs can really minimize the stress associated with incontinence especially when other things have been unsuccessful.

Changes in diet can also help bladder incontinence. Decreasing irritating fluids such as coffee, tea and soda improves urgency and frequency. For some people acidic drinks and foods such as citrus or tomato juices can irritate the bladder. Spicy foods can be a problem for both bowel and bladder irritation. High blood sugars also increase urgency for both bowel and bladder. And, finally, even though it seems a little counter-intuitive, dehydration can increase both the urgency and frequency of urination, because the concentrated urine is irritating to the bladder. Many people with urinary incontinence become dehydrated because they don't want to have "an accident," but this ends up causing more problems for the bladder and for their overall well-being.

There are many approaches to try to improve incontinence. People of any age don't have to just accept it. No matter what all those commercials from adult incontinence products say, being incontinent has serious impacts on the elderly and should be addressed.

Memory and Cognitive Decline

Not everyone experiences memory loss as they age. While cognitive processing speed does tend to naturally decrease over time, memory recall should not. Memory loss is not a normal part of aging, it is a complex disease process involving the brain. Not normal, but various diseases resulting in some form of dementia affects 14% of people over 70[vii].

As much as we joke about memory loss and getting older, let me repeat, memory loss is not a normal part of aging, it is part of one of many brain disease processes. Older adults are vulnerable to many of the diseases that affect memory and cognition. This section of the book could be its own book or even a whole series of books, because cognitive decline in adults has about 80 different causes. Alzheimer's disease is currently considered the most common cause of cognitive decline. Ok, am I using cognitive decline to be fancy instead of saying memory loss? No. No, because first memory loss is an overly simplistic explanation of what is happening to brain functions. Alzheimer's disease is multi-faceted. It can affect everything from the ability to make new memories, to emotions, coordination and the senses. Alzheimer's disease begins by causing more of an inability to make new memories than it does a loss of memories. This is why your grandfather with Alzheimer's disease can still tell you about his buddies in World War II, but he can't remember if he had lunch 15 minutes after lunch is over. It also seems to affect problem solving. So, your grandfather can remember you, but he might also believe that you are there to help him get his car keys back so he can drive even if he hasn't driven in years. And Alzheimer's affects senses so he might now like pouring ranch dressing all over his food, or sprinkling sugar on his cheeseburger, because otherwise it has no flavor to him. Or he may lose his ability to see the difference between the doorknob and the door. It is not so straight forward as simple loss of memory.

And Alzheimer's is just the beginning of a long list of brain diseases that cause "dementia" in the elderly. Dementia is a twisting of the thought processes. It is a catch-all phrase that only means that one person is not seeing the world the way most of us do. Cognitive decline, memory loss, personality changes, delusions and hallucinations are all related to brain diseases. Dementia or cognitive decline provides one of the biggest challenges to families, friends and professionals in caring for the elderly, because so much of who a person is and how a relationship works is in and from the mind.

Loved ones often feel like the person with dementia is not the same as the person they knew. They might say "this isn't my mom" or "this isn't my grandfather." When the mind changes we have a great deal of difficulty recognizing and accepting the person we knew and loved. As a nurse, that has always been hard for me to accept. Just between us, I didn't say this to families as it might feel hurtful, but I will share this here while you might have time to consider it. When you were born, you didn't know your mother, you didn't know her name, even as a young child you might have mistaken another woman for your mother. I remember holding on to a stranger's leg as a young girl thinking it was my mother I was trying to stay close to. The stranger and my mother laughed. When you were a teenager, you probably acted like a jerk at some point (I know I did.) and hopefully, your parent didn't say "you aren't my child anymore." Most parents and grandparents just continue to love and accept us through the many changes and stages in life. So, maybe it is your turn to love and accept them for who they are now, with dementia, whether they remember your name or not. Love and compassion are transcendent, and you can still get through to someone with dementia and let them know in the moment that you are there for them. So, if you had loving and accepting parents or grandparents who now don't quite know who you are or are being jerks, remember that they have experienced the same things with you.

Here is a brief explanation of the challenges that seniors might face when they (and you) are dealing with diseases of the brain.

Mild cognitive impairment – this diagnosis is provided to describe an inability to solve complex problems – not like chemical equations, but more like managing bills, appointments and finances. Timing meal preparations in a coherent way like they could in the past, or driving in unfamiliar territory. This does not tell you the underlying cause of the problem, if it will continue to decline or what to expect in the future. It's just a catch-all that a doctor or other healthcare provider might use to acknowledge that someone is having trouble cognitively.

Dementia, again, is another catch all term that describes more severe cognitive decline. It might also include personality changes, delusions, memory loss, or an inability to logically think through problems. Dementia does not mean much in terms of an understanding of an underlying disease process or diagnosis, nor does it help people understand a prognosis, or prediction of the future path of the disease. It is just an acknowledgement that the person is experiencing changes in his or her brain. I feel like this diagnosis is akin to someone diagnosing your loved one with pain. "Yep, your grandma's in pain. Take these pills." If that answer would be acceptable, then the diagnosis of "dementia" is acceptable. If not, ask to dig deeper. Why does grandma have dementia? What is causing it? Will it get worse? Stay the same? Get better? A better diagnosis is possible, and it can drive the type of treatment and outlook for life. It is worth investigating.

Alzheimer's Disease

Alzheimer's disease has two main categories: early onset and late onset. Early onset Alzheimer's is diagnosed before age 65 and has a strong hereditary component. Late onset Alzheimer's becomes apparent after 65 and is most common in people over 80. Both early and late on-set Alzheimer's have similar characteristics in the brain with proteins gumming up the internal workings of the cells and the erosion of the links between the brain cells. As cells are affected, they die and the brain deteriorates, becomes smaller and less connected. I know this is a simplistic explanation, if you want to talk about beta-amyloid and tau proteins, I suggest you look at more medical texts. I just want to help people reading this book translate and understand why things are going wrong in the brain.

Alzheimer's begins by affecting the ability to make memories, but it will affect the entire brain if it continues on its normal course. Many of us experience the inability to make memories from time to time. This usually stems from not focusing on what we are doing. My usual personal example looks like this: after work, I need to take one daughter to soccer practice and one daughter to gymnastics and stop at the grocery and the bank. While running through these errands, I'm also thinking about something that happened at work. On my third stop, the one to the grocery, I park, shop, come outside and have absolutely no idea where I parked. I have no ideas because I was busy and distracted and took no moment to make a memory of the location. Thankfully, this is not dementia or Alzheimer's disease. This is stress and distraction.

As Alzheimer's disease progresses from the inability to make memories, to the additional burdens of not being able to retrieve most old memories. In addition, Alzheimer's disease and other dementias may cause a phenomenon called confabulation. In confabulation, a person takes a part of a memory and mixes it with other things in their mind such as a movie or television show or a dream. This can lead to some disturbing narratives both for the victim of Alzheimer's and their caregivers. It may result in wild accusations or beliefs about people that aren't true such as believing that a staff member murdered someone or that a husband is having an affair with someone on tv.

Ultimately, Alzheimer's progresses to not being able to use tools in ways that we once did without thinking (such as keys, silverware, walkers) and then ultimately the body cannot coordinate well enough to do things like walk, talk or chew and swallow correctly. If Alzheimer's disease progresses it is fatal. However, most elderly people will die from other diseases or conditions prior to Alzheimer's taking its final toll.

Although this is not how the disease progresses in the brain, in my experience, having a loved one with Alzheimer's disease is like having their brain continually encased in more and more layers of barrier like layers of cotton batting. But there are keys to getting through even for the most severely affected. John Zeisel's concept and book *I'm Still Here*[viii] is a great way to think about living with and loving people with Alzheimer's. It may be harder and harder to get through, but keep trying and you will find your loved one beneath the layers. They may not know your name, but they will recognize your love and friendship. With many people with Alzheimer's it is as if they can meet your soul. They are also very sensitive to other's moods, feelings and discomfort. Alzheimer's is tough, as are all types of dementia, but my experience making connections with people with Alzheimer's have been some of the most meaningful and even joyful of my life and career. So, while people live in dread of getting an Alzheimer's diagnosis for themselves or their loved ones, please try to remember that there can still be good in their lives.

I want to relay one of my experiences with Alzheimer's over the years. In most of my examples, I use pseudonyms, but after talking with the husband of one of my patients, we decided to use real names in this story to relay some of the long road and reality of early-onset Alzheimer's. Over several years, I got to know Kim and her husband David. Kim was diagnosed with early on-set Alzheimer's. Kim and David went through many attempts to try to figure out what was wrong with her. At first, she had trouble with depression, with vision, and with her work. She didn't have a family history of early-onset Alzheimer's so there were no real warnings. By the time I met Kim and David, she was moving into our assisted living community. Their rural ranch home was not feasible for Kim anymore. David had to keep working and Kim couldn't be alone anymore. So he moved to a town with a good senior care community and to be near his sister for support, and Kim moved in with us in assisted living. Kim was physically healthy and resilient. She had been a runner and a tri-athlete. Kim still had the drive to exercise and be active. We helped her go swimming in our facility's pool. In addition to the assisted living staff, Kim had an extra private caregiver who took her on hikes, and other outings. Sometimes, Kim would forget why her husband wasn't living with her and become very sad and angry with him. Kim and I hit it off from the beginning. We all consoled her as best we could. One of the staff members sang to her in French, because she had been a French teacher, and he was from a French-speaking part of Africa. When that didn't work or provided just temporary relief, I would bring her into my office and turn on '70s rock and roll. We sat around like old friends, listening to music, maybe having a hot cocoa, and Kim could calm down. Kim and I bonded and when she was angry or confused, I would walk up and greet her warmly and she would relax and sometimes just say "Oh." Like, "Oh, it's you, my friend." It meant so much to me to be able to bring her comfort, even if over the 3 years I helped her, she never knew my name. After a while, Kim needed that French-speaking caregiver to sing to her while he fed her, because she couldn't concentrate on food or see her plate well enough. So, although she was less and less able, that connection continued. Our connection changed throughout her time as well, but she always seemed to be able to relax when I was with her. In our own way, we were friends even though she never really knew who I was or why I was there.

When Kim was passing away on Hospice, no longer able to walk, eat, or talk. We took turns sitting by her bed with her family. I could no longer see if I brought her any comfort, but I continued to try to share my heart with her and be by her side. I had the great honor of being there until the end of her life, and although I never knew the Kim that her family and husband knew, I was so glad that she had been part of my life and I had been part of hers. I was also glad to see an end to Kim and David's long difficult road.

So, when you think it is the end of the world when your loved one doesn't know your name or doesn't remember if you are his sister or his daughter or his wife, remember that you can still be a comfort and joy to them and you can connect with them.

Vascular Dementia

Vascular dementia stems from a lack of blood flow to all or part of the brain. The most common type involves brain changes after a stroke (or CVA). Because of the randomness of where a stroke affects the brain, the effects of a stroke can create very different types of changes depending on the location. One person might have an affected arm, another might lose sight or the ability to speak. If a stroke is in the front part of the brain, a person may lose the ability to reason or understand social situations and cues.

Until recently, medical professionals thought that the damage caused by strokes was irreversible. Thankfully that is not true in all cases. Recovery from strokes is a long, slow and difficult process, but many improvements can be made. The brain is much more adaptable than we used to believe. "Neuroplasticity" or the ability of the brain to adapt is an encouraging and growing field of research that brings hope to people dealing with brain injuries[ix]. Do not assume that the immediate effect, or even the effect that shows after several months, is the end result of a stroke. With time and therapy, the effects from a stroke can greatly diminish.

Another similar issue is the mini-stroke or transient ischemic attack (TIA). TIA's cause stroke like symptoms but they diminish within 24 hours. Over time, multiple TIAs can damage the brain and cause cognitive decline. I discussed this earlier in the book, but let me repeat. In the moment, people will not be able to tell what is a serious stroke and what is a mini-stroke or TIA. Please, get medical help immediately. No one will think you are over-reacting if the symptoms go away in the emergency room or (like is my frequent experience) as soon as the ambulance arrives. TIAs need to be investigated whenever they occur.

Vascular dementia can also be caused by difficulties with blood flow from the heart to the brain. Health issues such as high cholesterol, hardening of the arteries (artherosclerosis), smoking or diabetes can all damage the blood flow to the brain, depriving cells of oxygen and nutrition for functioning. If someone does not have a strong heart the lack of blood flow to the brain can decrease its capacity and cause cognitive decline.

Vascular dementia is not very systematic in nature. It all depends on the location and extent of the brain injury. One person may have more problems with finding words, another might have more difficulty with complex decisions and still another may lose their ability to understand social cues or lose their social inhibitions. Also, people are sometimes diagnosed with "mixed dementia" which is often a result of vascular dementia in addition to Alzheimer's disease or some other type of dementia.

Parkinson's Disease and Lewy Body Dementia

Parkinson's disease is a progressive neurological disease that primarily affects movement, but is also associated with depression, labile or unstable cognitive problems and constipation. Half to three-quarters of people diagnosed with Parkinson's disease gets Lewy Body Dementia (LBD). [xxi] Like Alzheimer's, LBD is caused by a protein that gums up the brain cells. This type of dementia tends to come with more emotional/mental health problems, and has an increased risk of paranoia, auditory and visual hallucinations. Dealing with a loved one with LBD can be especially difficult and it is important to get help both for the person affected and his or her loved ones. The most prominent victim of LBD and its mental health impacts is comedian Robin Williams. Williams ended his own life in 2014 while suffering depression, anxiety and paranoia associated with Parkinson's Disease and LBD. LBD affects men more than women, and the men I have worked with have an unrelenting restlessness that accompanies this disease. This restlessness means that they tend to have more risks of injuries. So, the risk of falls, wandering off, or being injured because he is dismantling the television, wheelchair, or table (again) is significant. Hallucinations can be frightening – such as seeing snakes or scary people or they can be quizzically interesting. I worked with one woman who would look out onto the patio and happily say, "Look at those monkeys out there!" She was not at all disturbed by the monkeys, so we, as staff members, just went along with it. "Huh, go figure, aren't they cute?" Which brings me to another aspect of hallucinations. You cannot talk people out of their hallucinations and you will end up either making them really angry or scaring them. "Look, Mom, there are no snakes on the floor. See I'm standing right here and there are no snakes!" This will be followed by, "Oh dear god, don't stand with the snakes! Be careful! Get out of there! Why can't you see the snakes? Are you stupid? Are you calling me crazy?" No amount of reality orientation will convince someone with hallucinations that they do not exist. It is better to find something to reassure the person. "I'll let the snakes out of the room, and you can stay in bed until they go away." Or, if you are not that creative, reassure the person hallucinating that you are going to keep her safe. "I'll take care of you." As a nurse, working with people with dementia-related hallucinations, I sometimes feel like an actor in some kind of improv theater that I don't understand. As I am trying to calm someone with hallucinations, I am playing along and picking up items off the floor that do not actually exist, or I escort invisible people out the door to relieve a patient's fear.

Sometimes it is hard to know if someone is serious about their hallucinations. Recently, I was working with a resident who was constantly taking off his pants and underwear, and making the caregivers a little uncomfortable. I went into his room to deliver something for him and there he was – naked. I will call him Abuelo – the Spanish word for grandfather. I said, "Abuelo! Cover up, I don't want to see that." He apologized, but then in his mixed Spanish and English he told me, "The cucarachas, they eat my clothes." And I laughed, "Oh Abuelo, I don't think so." He was so mad at me. I thought he was kidding. But he really did hallucinate cockroaches, and believed they were in his clothes. So…bad move by the experienced nurse. I didn't catch on to the hallucination, and was blaming this man for knowingly undressing and making the staff uncomfortable when that was not the case. Live and learn! It's easy for any of us to not understand someone else's hallucinations. But, it's best if we can adjust quickly and adapt to their reality.

Frontal Lobe Dementia

Frontal Lobe Dementia affects, you guessed it, the frontal lobe of the brain. This large section of the brain controls problem solving, impulse control, attention, social and moral reasoning, motor control, mood, personality, sexual behavior, and problem solving.[xii] This is the last part of the brain to fully develop in humans. Adolescents are in the process of developing this part of the brain, and any of us who have been or have parented adolescents know that this can be a trying period. If the frontal lobe of the brain is deteriorating, people have trouble with socializing and impulse control. Seniors with frontal lobe dementia may remember a lot of things (although sometimes memory is also affected) but they may have more significant personality changes.

This type of dementia can be hard on families, and especially on those who have had difficult relationships in the past. Elders affected by FLD can say mean and inappropriate things to loved ones, caretakers and even the person on the street. FLD can cause major and intractable mood changes causing constant tearfulness or anxiety. Let's be honest FLD is tough. Especially if you don't know what is going on because your loved one does not have an accurate or clear diagnosis. It is hard to understand why mom has suddenly turned on you or is calling dad foul names that she never would have in the past. This is a good place to talk about knowing your limits. Short visits and trying not to have your feelings hurt can be important. People with FLD can say some really harsh or untrue things such as "your sister is my favorite" or "look how big your butt is." If you can, it's best to try to have a thick skin and a sense of humor. Also with FLD, the combination of reduced impulse control and declining motor function makes the risk of falls and other accidents very high. There are different devices that might help with potential falls or unsafe movement. These usually involve alarms from sensors that go off with standing or getting out of bed. Although used frequently in care settings, unless staff or loved ones are close, they mostly let you know that someone is already on the floor, and are going out of fashion in care settings.

Acting out sexually by masturbating frequently, and sometimes in public or by making sexual comments to or inappropriate touching of caregivers can cause serious issues for others. Sexual behavior can be acceptable if it is welcome attention or doesn't bother others, or it can impact the rights of others. Caregivers need to feel safe around their patients, so working to limit sexual aggression by patients is an important part of care planning. This is sometimes done by providing caregivers that are not subject to this unwanted attention (such as a male caregiver for a heterosexual male patient). Other times, two caregivers have to work with a sexually aggressive patient to help redirect hands and attention or just to make the care staff feel more comfortable.

Treatment for FLD usually includes physical therapy for motor control and use of medications such as anti-depressants and anti-psychotics including controversial medications such as olanzapine, risperdol, quetiapine or haldol. Use of these types of anti-psychotics is controversial due to the association with falls and death, but they can help if behaviors are so severe that the sufferer is at risk of harming himself or others. In the past, anti-psychotics were over-used to control elderly patients instead of using other non-pharmalogical interventions such as redirection or reassurance. In any case, minimal dosing should be used if anti-psychotics are needed to alleviate troubling hallucinations or delusions.

To illustrate some of the difficulties with frontal lobe dementia behaviors, I will share one of my experiences in a specialized dementia care unit.

I was sitting with a woman who was in her final hours in a memory care where I worked. She and I had been through a lot together, and I was trying to reconcile those difficulties with the now harmless lady lying in bed with irregular breathing and no more words to say. She had been a difficult resident to love in my time with her. She was extremely sexually aggressive with the male caregivers grabbing their crotches and behinds and asking them to get in the shower with her. She had tried to perform oral sex on another resident in the middle of the common area before staff intervened. We had to limit her care from the staff from African and African American caregivers, because she would call them the N-word. As I sat with her putting lotion on her hands, her adult children came in. They began talking about their mother with a great deal of love. I said something like, "Was she always a feisty lady?" And they said, "Oh no, our mom was so sweet and loving. So kind." Luckily I had worked in memory care long enough to hone my generic, non-committal response, and said something like, "Isn't that great?" We hadn't really told the family the extent of our struggles with her. Her life with FLD had obviously been quite different from her family life. I'm just glad she is at peace now and that her family could still see their mother as the sweet and kind woman she had been.

Although there are 80 different, specific types of dementia, I am just covering the most frequent here. Diagnosing dementia is not an exact science with a living patient (examining the brain is the best determination), but physicians and other experienced health care providers can make fairly accurate diagnosis with tests and examination. Getting a specific diagnosis will help you understand the path your loved one is on. It will also help you and your loved one cope with the changes, and provide a solid foundation for physicians to prescribe medication if needed.

Medication Management

Most older adults take medications to help with chronic diseases such as high blood pressure, diabetes, digestive problems, cholesterol, chronic pain, mood etc. Some medications are effective in managing diseases and symptoms, and some have limited usefulness. Medication usefulness should always be weighed against the extent of the problem, and the effectiveness of the drug. Twenty five percent of people 65-69 take five prescriptions drugs. Forty six percent of people between 70 and 79 take at least five prescription drugs.[xiii] This does not account for over-the-counter medicines or supplements. Medications can be helpful or hurtful or sometimes both. Sometimes medications have side effects that are harmful or bothersome, but the need outweighs the harm done. For instance an antibiotic for pneumonia might cause nausea, but it is worth taking the medication. But a medication for osteoporosis costing thousands of dollars that may damage the digestive tract but only increases bone density by less than 2%…well, I wouldn't buy it. Weigh the pros and cons of medications carefully. Polypharmacy (the combined negative effects of medications and supplements) creates major problems for seniors.

Often, confusion exists regarding which medications to take and for how long. This is especially true if someone goes to multiple physicians or health care providers, and is even more true if a senior does not have a coordinating primary care doctor, good records, and a trusted pharmacist.

For example, a patient may go to an urgent care or emergency room for a fall and be prescribed a pain reliever. This might be meant for a few days, but somehow it gets added to the medication list and the drug keeps getting prescribed when it isn't really needed. Or, an elderly person may need something to protect his/her stomach while in the hospital on strong antibiotics, but then doesn't need it later. Yet somehow that drug ends up on a medication list that follows the person to a skilled nursing facility and then home. Two years later, someone might wonder why this person is using it. But it could just go on and on unnecessarily.

In addition, medications that might be effective earlier in life – like a cholesterol lowering drug – aren't effective later in life. Or, a medication prescribed for depression after the loss of a spouse may not be necessary after a normal grieving process. Medications should be reviewed at least every six months to make sure there are not unnecessary drugs on the list. This can be done with a doctor, health care provider or pharmacist. Nurses can also help with this process and make recommendations, although nurses cannot prescribe medication.

With the increase in advertising for medications, please be mindful that for a medication to be considered effective, it doesn't have to help very much. For example, a very expensive injection for osteoporosis makes a difference in stopping bone loss – but only by a small percentage. So, is a $1500 injection twice a year to slow bone loss by a few percentage points worth taking? A newer diabetes medication is considered more effective because it lowers blood sugar by 1.1% to 1.4%. It costs $600 per month at least it did the last time I checked, no doubt this price will increase by the time you read this book. So you have to determine if that is worth the small change in blood sugar. If a drug is considered "effective" by a drug company, it's best to check and see by how much.

Medications can be one of the hardest things for independent seniors to manage, and mixing up medications can have serious consequences. Assistance managing medications falls into three main categories: Reminders, packaging and administration.

Reminders can be done by the phone or in person by family or friends that stop in daily. Alternatively, a timer or watch alarm can be set. And the plethora of electronics that we now use can help. I work with one gentlemen who takes Parkinson's medicine. This medicine has to be taken at very precise times, many times per day. His nephew set up Amazon's Alexa to remind him and it is working really well!

Packaging can also help. Medicine bottle labels can be made with large print for easier reading. Medi-sets (the long plastic boxes with a compartment for every day of the week) can be set up with pills for each day. "Salad packs" are packages with the day and time a group of medications should be given. (Think of a tossed salad of pills.) All of these packaging options can be set up by either mail order or local pharmacies for a small additional fee.

Special packaging also includes some newer products that dispense medications at certain times. A variety of these systems come with different levels of monitoring and times per day. Of course, the price tags also differ. These range from $100 to $1500. The higher end models can even send someone else a text if medications are not taken on time. The cost might be higher, but it is a lot less than administration by a home care agency or in a senior living setting which will cost more than $500 per month.

Medication regimes can be really complicated – such as the Parkinson's medications that I referenced above. However, if medications are fairly simple, and you need more help than set up and reminders then there might be other unmet needs. So consider having one or two people who are really good at coordinating stop by and administer medications. Make sure you have back up so if someone wants or needs a break, the system doesn't fall apart. The next option would be to hire a home care agency to assist with medications. This might be especially helpful if an elder needs more help. For example, medication assistance plus meal preparation and a safety check might be worth a try.

As you consider a move into a senior living community, medication administration is an additional charge to rent and meals. Also, when someone is a resident in a licensed care facility a significant number of rules about medications come into play. Nurses and aides have to have signed orders from a doctor for healthcare provider or any medication or supplement. These orders have to be precise – if a doctor orders one regular strength Tylenol every 6 hours for arthritis pain, the nurse or aide can't give two, or give an extra strength. If you buy Calcium tablets for your mother to take, they have to match the dosage written by the physician exactly. The increase in vigilance and adherence to rules for medications can be a good thing, but it can also be a headache: A headache for which you cannot have an aspirin until the physician orders one.

In addition to how medications are packaged and handled, all seniors should have a method of keeping track of what they have been prescribed, what they take and how often they take it. Carrying a list with you will help keep this handy if you need to assist your loved one with a medical appointment or emergency. Below is a template of how this might look. Details in this list, such as dosages, are very important for keeping your loved one safe.

Follow these tips to keep a reliable and safe effective list of medications:

- Make a list of routine medications including the name, dose, and frequency. (See examples after the list of tips)
- Make a list of allergies. (See examples after the list of tips)
- Take these lists to ANY and EVERY health care appointment – this includes eye doctors, dentists, therapy, etc.
- Destroy old medications including those that are expired or that are no longer prescribed. This prevents the temptation of adding an old medication back into the mix when someone doesn't think the current medications are working,

and can also prevent theft or unwanted use by others with access to the medicine cabinet.

- Use one pharmacy.
- Ask the pharmacist to review your medication list, and tell you and your doctor if she/he has any concerns. Pharmacists can be very helpful and they are an under-utilized resource!
- Try to have one primary doctor or health care provider (like a nurse practitioner).
- If a specialist, such as a cardiologist prescribes something, ask the medical office to let your primary care doctor know, and follow up with your primary care provider to make sure it is done.
- Take medications as prescribed. If medications aren't working for you – say they make you nauseous or you don't feel like they are effective – call the prescriber and let them know. It's better than fiddling around with the dosing yourself.

Medication	Dose	Frequency	Reason
Acetaminophen	325 mg capsule	3 times a day	Joint pain
Levothyroxine	75 mcg tablet	In the morning	Hypothyroid
Multivitamin with minerals	1 tablet	One time a day	Supplement
Citalopram	20 mg tablet	One time a day at bedtime	Grief

| Melatonin | 3 mg tablets | Occasionally at bed time | Insomnia |

Example Medication List

Allergen	Category	Reaction
Penicillin	Drug	Had hives as a kid
Shrimp	Food	Hives and couldn't breathe
Ragweed	Environmental	Sneezing

Example Allergy List

To provide you with an example of how things can get mixed up with multiple doctors and pharmacists if we aren't paying attention, I will tell you one of my many encounters with polypharmacy. Just today, as I was reviewing medications for an elderly lady, she had the following medications on her list (and these were being taken every day):

- Ocuvite – one daily (a multivitamin that includes specific minerals and Omega 3 for eye health)
- I-vite – one daily (a multivitamin that includes specific minerals for eye health)
- Women's multivitamin with minerals – one daily
- Theravite multivitamin with minerals – one daily
- Omega 3 capsules 4 per day

Either the physicians have some master plan that includes taking 4 different multivitamins with minerals, or each time a physician saw the patient s/he wrote the prescription slightly differently and sent it to the pharmacy so that the patient ended up on four different multivitamins and an additional supplement that is already in one of the multivitamins. Hopefully no harm was done, but this is just one example of the problems that can arise if medications are not reviewed.

Medical Procedures

Elderly or not, we should all approach medical procedures with some caution. Not because we should be overly concerned about malpractice or terrible outcomes, but because invasive procedures usually come with a host of side effects, and the possibility that the procedure is minimally helpful. If possible, take time to weigh alternatives to surgical procedures. If there are options to surgery, consider those first. Physical therapy or other long term treatments might be just as helpful as surgery.

For example, years ago, I had pelvic pain from endometriosis, I had a lysis of adhesions. This outpatient procedure removed scar tissue through laparoscopy (a procedure done with a scope and very small incisions), and it did help for a while. However, *after* the surgery, my doctor let me know that for people with adhesions the procedure itself can cause the body to create more scar tissue. So, the more surgery I had, the more scar tissue I would have. In hindsight, I'm not sure I should have had the surgery at all. It may have eventually made things worse. A decade later I had a hysterectomy and during this procedure, the same surgeon found lots more scar tissue had built up in the same locations as my last surgery.

It isn't a simple decision to have an invasive medical procedure. For the elderly and probably everyone else, additions to the usual questions should be:

- What anesthesia will be needed?
- What will recovery include?
- How much will this help the problem?
- What kinds of medications will I need afterward?

For the elderly, additional considerations have to be weighed.

- Will your loved one participate in therapy for recovery? For example, will she/he participate in physical therapy after a hip replacement?
- Will your loved one be able to go back home after a procedure? You don't want to find out after mom has had a knee replacement that the hospital wants to discharge her to a nursing facility for 6 weeks. Ask about plans for therapy and recovery, and if it will involve a stay in a nursing or rehabilitation facility.
- Will the surgery improve quality of life?
- Will it increase longevity?
- Do you want increased longevity?

Increasing the length of life may not always feel like the best plan. Quality of life definitely needs to be considered.

If your loved one is 90 and they want to aim for 105, that is fine. I'm not judging his desire for a longer life. You just need to have that conversation. We see a lot of surgeries on people with diseases like Alzheimer's and Parkinson's Disease. Sometimes these surgeries enhance the long trajectory of the illness and lengthen suffering. Try to find a physician who wants to look at the big picture and not just their surgical specialty.

Here, I want to continue my earlier discussion of Kim, who had early-onset Alzheimer's and her husband, Dave. When Dave's wife was showing signs of early-onset Alzheimer's disease, she developed breast cancer. Dave took her to appointments for testing and diagnosis. He went through the process of helping plan for a mastectomy. The doctors and surgeons planned and proceeded with the mastectomy. Dave tells me "not one time did anyone say 'Hey, Dave! Have you thought about this? Your wife probably has Alzheimer's. Do you want to go through the suffering of surgery and breast cancer treatment so that you can extend her suffering from Alzheimer's?'" Don't expect that medical professionals will put surgery and other procedures in the context of the big picture of other disease processes. Often, it seems, that they believe that you have done the hard work of thinking through the ethical implications of medical procedures. Especially when it comes to specialties, doctors tend to stay within their comfort zone.

So, for example let's say your great uncle lives at home and has developed an irregular heartbeat. His cardiologist recommends surgical placement of a pacemaker. Considering whether it will improve his quality of life. It may not if your uncle doesn't notice the irregular heartbeat, isn't feeling faint or is not very active. It may just be a precaution. Here is an example of the types of questions you should consider:

Questions	Answers
What are the risks of the surgery?	Infection, limited movement in his left arm, pain
Will he need therapy or long-term care after surgery?	No, he will have outpatient surgery and go home.
Will he need any new medications after the surgery?	He may need pain medicine and an antibiotic.
Will the surgery increase longevity?	Yes, it probably will help him live longer because having an irregular heartbeat increases the risk of strokes, and other damage to the heart
Does he want to increase longevity?	Well, not really. He has been a widow for 6 years. He has terrible osteoarthritis that causes a lot of pain, and he has lived a long and fulfilling life. He has told you before that he is ready to "go home."

Example Questions for Pacemaker

Another example might be that your 88-year old aunt has broken her hip. Surgery will require a hip replacement.

Here is an example of similar questions and answers in this scenario:

Questions	Answers
Will she need therapy or long-term care after surgery?	Yes, she will be discharged to a skilled nursing or rehabilitation facility and receive daily therapy for 4-6 weeks, then she will have in-home therapy twice a week for 6 more weeks.
Is she the kind of person who will participate in therapy?	Yes, she has gone to physical therapy before and saw how it helped her.
Will she need different medications?	Yes, she will need antibiotics, narcotic pain management and a stomach acid reducer.
Will surgery increase longevity?	Yes, the fracture will cause pain and limited mobility, likely shortening her life.
Does she want to increase longevity?	Yes, her mother lived to be 102, and your aunt loves to walk with her friends and takes her great niece out in the stroller twice a week then has dinner at your house. She doesn't have a lot of medical problems and she has no memory or cognitive problems. The surgery will have risks and it will require her to slow down and take a lot of physical therapy, but the chance is definitely worth the risk and rehabilitation.

Example Questions for Hip Replacement

Anesthesia, Surgery and Dementia: Special Considerations

How might anesthesia affect the patient after surgery? Cognitive decline is very common after a surgical procedure. Everyone gets groggy and a little confused after anesthesia, but it takes a long time to clear anesthesia when your older body processes are slower and you may have lower kidney function to help clear the anesthesia. In addition, for some reason, elderly people do not always completely recover. If an elder already has some dementia, the effects of surgery, anesthesia, time in the hospital and recovery can be devastating. If your loved one ends up needing to go to the hospital remember, hospitals are very confusing, and you should expect some strange behaviors during a hospital stay. Expect to have a close friend or family member stay at the hospital with an elderly loved one to reassure them, and make sure they are safe. And remember, hospitals in the US exist to treat an acute problem, and then get that patient transferred out as soon as possible due to insurance and other payment options. So, know that even if your grandfather is 99, the hospital protocols will push to treat him and get him released. Don't get mad at the staff for waking him up for the next round of antibiotics or taking his vital signs. In our current system, patients are not in the hospital to rest. People are in the hospital for acute care and to be released for further recovery. We can argue about whether or not this hospital system is the best we can do, but I'm just telling you how it will be.

Long hospital stays have been replaced with rehabilitation centers in skilled nursing facilities for care. In addition, during the discharge process an elderly patient will often be given the option of going to skilled nursing (or a nursing home) to complete recovery and receive daily therapy. These stays may be two to six weeks long. They can be helpful in getting your loved one back on his/her feet before returning home.

As an illustration of hospitals and anesthesia affects on elders, I want to share one of my experiences.

Early in my career taking care of people with Alzheimer's I took care of a pleasant, but confused resident, Bette, who fell in our main dining room and broke her hip. She was usually up walking, talking, and eating meals with gusto (she loved to eat.) A few days after her fracture and hip replacement surgery I went to visit her at the hospital. Bette was in wrist and ankle restraints. The hospital staff had tied her to the bed with restraints, because she kept climbing over the side rails. Despite the pain of the hip replacement, she was so confused that she had pulled out IVs and was attempting to escape. They had even tried having a family member there, but she was very quick to pull IVs out. They resorted to both strong anti-anxiety medication and physical restraints.

In later years, I worked with another elder lady, Sally, who had some vascular dementia, but usually knew who she was and where she was. However, when I visited her in the hospital after she fell, broke her arm and had surgery, she was pretty convinced that she had just had a baby. She was letting everyone know (including her quite embarrassed grandson) that this wasn't her first rodeo because she had three other children, and they didn't need to make such a fuss about giving birth.

Safety

When my grandfather was 87, he fell off a ladder cleaning his gutters. Luckily, he just had some bruises and a sore back. Gramps loved his small farm and home, and he always worked on the garden and property. At least when he wasn't hiring one of his five granddaughters during the hot Ohio summers to "help." I'm not sure we were much help, but Gramps gave us pocket money, and we got to spend time with him mowing fields, painting the metal roof and probably causing more trouble than we were worth. At 87, it had not occurred to me that Gramps would think it was ok to climb a ladder to clean his own gutters. I knew he still mowed the grass and that my grandmother was upset about that. She didn't want him to die mowing the lawn, but knowing how much he loved taking care of the place, I thought it wouldn't be a bad way to die – doing something you love. Obviously, we had different ideas about what was safe and what wasn't. Like many loyal grandchildren, I probably still truly felt that he was invincible.

I tell this story to illustrate that like beauty, safety is in the eye of the beholder. The trade-off of some safety measures is the freedom to live and do what you want. Moving my grandfather out of his farm house would have eliminated the risk of mowing his lawn or cleaning his gutters. Goodness knows, he, like many people, wasn't just going to stop doing those things because we asked. When all this was going on I was finishing my graduate degree and then beginning my career in California. So, I wasn't much help. I know my parents helped him manage chores, but they couldn't be there all the time and I'm pretty sure that my independent grandfather wouldn't have wanted them to be.

So the trade-offs of some safety questions are tricky. Making people 99% safe from something like a fall is no problem. You just tie them into their chair, and probably give them some drugs to keep them docile. However, that is not the model we use (at least not anymore.) Where do you draw the line? This is another area that needs discussion and consideration from an elder and his/her loved ones. In addition, if a senior is in a licensed residential facility, they cannot just let them be unsafe because an elderly person wants to take the risk. Falls and accidents can affect the licenses of senior living facilities, so there may be an additional layer of negotiation on top of what you have already decided.

Here are the things that seem to be family's biggest worries for senior safety:

- Will they fall?
- Will they fall and not be able to get help?
- Will they take the wrong medicine?
- Will they get scammed?
- Will they have a fire at home?
- Will they get into a car accident?

Falls can be decreased by working in two directions: first focusing on the environment, and second, simultaneously working on the body's strength, flexibility and balance. Changing the environment starts with a home survey. You can do this using some common sense and observation, or you can use a qualified nurse, occupational therapist, or physical therapist. Most seniors can get a physical therapy or occupational therapy consult in their homes with a referral from a physician, nurse practitioner or other health care provider. Therapists are great resources, and can identify potential hazards for mobility that you might not consider. Just remember to actually follow-up on their recommendations. Physical therapists and occupational therapists can also help seniors adapt and strengthen their bodies to reduce fall risks. Whether a senior is at home or in a residential care facility, these therapists will slowly work to help them strengthen muscles that improve balance and gait (the way they walk). The other way of working on the body is to check if medications might be increasing fall risk. If a medication that increases fall risk can be decreased or replaced, try it. Most commonly the medications that increase fall risk are blood pressure medications, diuretics (water pills), mood stabilizers (such as anti-anxiety, anti-psychotics or some anti-depressants), sleep aides, and narcotic pain relievers. As I talk about in the section on medications, make sure you have these reviewed to see if they are necessary, and being used in the right dosage.

Common medications that may increase fall risk	
Blood Pressure	Lisinopril Enalapril Carvedilol Metoprolol Toprol
Mood Stabilizers	Lorazepam Xanax Seroquel Quetiapine Older anti-depressants – amitryptiline, Doxepin
Diuretics	Lasix Furosemide Spironolactone Hydrochlorothiazide
Anti-histamines	Benadryl Hydroxizine
Incontinence control	Oxybutynine Myrbetriq Vesicare
Narcotic pain relievers	Oxycodone Hydrocodone Morphine Tramadol

As far as falling and not being able to get up, well, we have all seen the commercial. You don't want your loved one to be the one yelling "I've fallen and I can't get up!" The simplest system is an emergency alert system that is always worn on the body. There are a lot of companies, like Life Alert, that provide this service. If you don't like that option, and your loved one can wear a watch with a phone in it, Apple watches and Gizmos from Verizon are options that may work, although Gizmos are designed for children, they are simple and effective. Other tech savvy elders may wear their cell phone in a pouch around their neck. The advantage to the medical emergency alert system is that they are simple, and that some of them detect falls themselves without the need for the person to call. Even if you have people checking in a few times a day, a fall could mean many hours on the floor waiting for help if a senior doesn't have an emergency alert system. Unfortunately, the biggest problem with these systems is resistance from the wearer. First, your loved one may resist wearing one. Second, they may resist using them after a fall. Vanity is not just for the young and (let's face it) middle-aged, often seniors don't like the feel of alert systems or don't like announcing to the world that they need them by wearing one all the time. The neck cords or wrist bands attached can be changed to make them more comfortable and fashionable. For the most fashion-forward seniors, feel free to go to the craft store and bling up the call buttons to suit their style. It won't affect the function and it may encourage them to wear the device more.

Cooking, Hot Water, Fires, Woodstoves, and Space Heaters

You can tell I am cooking by the sound of the smoke detectors going off in my house, so I am not here to judge anyone's cooking skills or really their ability to pay attention for any length of time, because, I generally do not have a long enough attention span to even make a grilled cheese sandwich without burning at least one side. If you are concerned about burns and fires, consider removing the need for cooking or heating systems that could cause a fire. Space heaters and wood stoves are notoriously dangerous, and need careful management. If your elder loved one can't manage these types of heaters, help them find alternatives. Setting up an automatic thermostat will help keep the house the right temperature during waking and sleeping hours without the need for space heaters. Don't give in to keeping the thermostat set at 90 degrees either. It might feel comfortable to a senior with little fat or and not enough movement or exercise, but it will still dehydrate them. Try to find a good compromise like mid-70s at the warmest.

Many alternatives exist to cooking. As much as I have traveled for work helping senior living communities in the past year, I could probably write a book on how to eat without ever actually cooking anything. Pre-made soups, salads and individual servings of fruits, vegetables and protein are available at any grocery store. Microwaves are safer options than open flames or electric burners, as long as they are place on counter level and not up high. Pre-made, one person meals have come a long way since foil-covered TV dinners. If you can help your loved one stock up on easy microwaveable meals that can be a big help.

There are also meal delivery services (Door Dash, Uber Eats as well as groups of neighbors and specific restaurants that deliver.) Unfortunately, the cost of these restaurant-based options is high (and the food is often high in calories). Meals-on-Wheels is a not-for-profit service in many areas of the US that is run by volunteers, they can provide regular daily, nutritious meals for the elderly who cannot get out, or cannot cook meals. Local senior centers can provide meals too. Senior centers also provide social time. These meals at senior centers usually aren't free, but they are cheap. The benefit of Meals-on-Wheels and senior center meals is that these programs are helpful in checking on people too, providing one more set of eyes on your loved one's well-being.

Financial Difficulties and Scams

Scamming has morphed into quite an art form. It seems that every month there is a new way of getting people to part with their money and private information. Telephones, the internet and door-to-door scams affect many seniors. Discussing security and scams is the first step to keeping your loved one safe from financial exploitation. Senior centers, the local police and organizations like the AARP and the National Council on Aging have up-to-date information on scams[xiv][xv]. Keep track of these and inform your loved one. It can also be beneficial to make sure that a trusted person can help monitor bank accounts to make sure there are not any unwanted withdrawals. Having a limited number of credit cards also makes it easier to keep track of money and account information. Ask your elder loved one for on-line access to monitor his or her account, or chose another trustworthy family-member to do so.

Seniors, like all of us, need to remember this absolute rule:

Never give any numbers to someone who calls you!

- No social security number.
- No account number.
- No address.
- No birthdate.
- No medicare number.

In sum, no numbers!

This means to be very protective, never buy, donate or pay bills over the phone if someone calls you. If you call an organization that you want to donate to, or you need to pay for a service that is different. Legitimate charities and businesses will provide other avenues for bills, donations and sales. There is no need to donate over the phone and this would violate absolute number one! One more time: Don't give any numbers to anyone who calls you!

If your senior loved one is using e-mail and other internet programs, help them identify types of scams like phishing for passwords and mimicking valid websites. Internet scams are getting more sophisticated and they are easy traps to fall into. The safeguard of having oversight over back accounts can be helpful.

If someone will not stop calling, visiting or e-mailing and trying to extract money or information, report them to the police. Reporting to the police does everyone a favor, by notifying and hopefully publicizing the types of financial scams that are occurring. Police often share information about scams to other members of the community so they can be aware.

Also, the unfortunate truth is that most financial exploitation is perpetrated by family members. For this reason, a trusted family member or two, or financial professional who has oversight of accounts can be very important. The scammer may not be a bogus roofing company knocking on the door, it may be a wayward daughter who decides to pad her own account with a senior's money.

Cars and Driving

Most United States cities are designed to navigate by personal car. Having and driving a car means freedom for many Americans. The idea of losing your driving privileges is devastating to many seniors. It may be difficult, but if drivers are no longer safe, action has to be taken. Children of seniors who have to encourage their parent to stop driving, have a tough job. When the children have to take charge, it changes the relationship drastically. The person laying down the rules is now the one who used to be beholden to them. Driving seems to be a real tipping point in the parent/child relationship. A bad driver, whether young or old, could hurt both himself and others. No one wants that.

You may have an argument that sounds like this:

- Grandma: There are a lot worse drivers than I am! What about all those kids on their phones? What about 16 year olds? What about bicyclists? Taxis? Last year when you ran that stop sign?
- You: Are there a lot of bad drivers out there? Yes. Are a lot of people distracted while driving? Yes, as a cyclist who can easily see into cars, I say YES! There are too many distracted drivers. But other bad drivers do not make you safer. It makes everyone unsafe. We want fewer unsafe drivers on the roads, not more.

If you want to know what to look for in determining whether someone is a safe driver, consider a senior's vision, ability to turn his/her head to look for traffic, hearing, reaction time, ability to lift and move his/her feet. If these things are in doubt, then the senior should be evaluated for safe driving. AARP conducts safe driving courses that might be enough to help evaluate abilities. If that is not an option, you can ask for an evaluation at a DMV. Or, if you know this is going to cause a huge conflict and potentially ruin any hope of future relationships, you can turn in unsafe drivers anonymously. For example in Washington State, the form is on-line.[xvi] Contact your local DMV or police to see if they can follow up with unsafe drivers.

In the meantime, offer pre-emptive rides to the store or to activities you know are important to help decrease reliance on a personal vehicle. Making an alternative readily available before the loss of driving privileges can help soften the blow.

Depression and Mental Illness

Symptoms of depression affect many elders. Combinations of neurological and chemical changes along with declining abilities and social isolation create a rich environment for depression to take hold and grow. In the United States, about 10% of adults have a diagnosis of depression, and many more people have depression that is undiagnosed and untreated. As anyone who suffers with depression knows, it creates a cycle that feeds on itself. Being depressed leads to a lack of initiative to do things such as socializing, exercising, being productive and taking action. Not socializing, exercising or having tasks and goals feeds depression. The losses people face more frequently in older age can lead to situational depression that can trigger the cycle to start. Loss of a best friend, a brother or sister, a spouse, and the loss of abilities, homes or activities can certainly weigh on a person. Add this to the other lifestyle and physiological changes and depression can easily begin. As the loved one of an elder with depression, this can be a frustrating cycle. You know that your aunt would benefit from going to the senior center for lunch or taking a walk, but you just cannot get her to do it. How can you help someone who won't (or can't) get out of the cycle and do something for their own well-being. It's maddening.

Be honest with your loved one. Talk to them about feeling sad or depressed. Make a plan and stick with it. Small steps towards social integration, time outside, enjoying old tasks or finding ways to engage in something that a senior cannot do in an old way can really help. For example, did your mother enjoy quilting when she was younger, but now she cannot do it because of a loss of dexterity or vision? Try attending a quilt show. Did your neighbor enjoy running in local 5k fun runs when he was younger, but his knees no longer allow him to even walk long distances? Help him volunteer at a track meet or a local fun run. There are many ways of engaging in things that once brought us joy if you think creatively.

Take me for example, for many years, I have enjoyed long distance biking, my family has ridden on multi-day trips in the US and Canada on rail trails, and we live very close to 27 glorious smooth miles of paved bike trails. I know that someday, I won't be able to or at least my kids will discourage me from riding a skinny tire road bike. Now, I look at recumbent bikes, trikes and other safer models and think "someday, I'm buying one of those." It will be an adaptation for when I may not be safe balancing a two wheeler. (Honestly, I'm not that coordinated now!) In one nursing facility I worked, we had a rickshaw that worked for wheelchairs. A staff member would pedal the trike and a resident would be in the back safely locked in while sitting in her wheelchair. They could ride the beautiful paved trails around the nursing home. While working there, I always thought "please use that for me if I am ever wheelchair bound." What a great piece of equipment to have! I will no longer be able to ride my bike someday, but I bet I would love to experience biking in a different way. Rethinking how to participate in long-time interests is an important way to stay engaged and lift people's spirits.

Many medications, such as sertraline or citalopram, exist to help people with chemical imbalances that cause depression. Usually, these medications can be safely used for seniors, and they may provide the boost they need to get back into life, and find more things they enjoy. However, as we reviewed earlier when discussing medications, because of the potential side effects of some anti-depressants, they should be re-evaluated every 6 months to determine if they are still needed.

In my experience, I have also found that many people deal with depression their whole lives, but it isn't treated. Once a senior starts getting a lot of clinical and medical attention, for example if they are admitted to an assisted living, the staff may become concerned about mental health issues. There are a few paths to take when this happens. As a nurse, I often hear "my mom has always had issues with being sad – she used to stay in her bedroom for a few days every couple of months when we were kids. It's just the way she is." So then you have to ask yourself: Is that the best for our mom? Should we try to get her help at 80 that she didn't at 40? I would suggest you take advantage of the extra medical attention your mom is getting at 80, and consider ways that might still benefit her. Talk to her and to the nurses and doctors about strategies to help. There is nothing wrong with working on a lifelong problem near the end of life. Mental illness, whether it starts at a late age or has been present for a long time inhibits peoples' well-being. Consider the options on what can be done.

Brain disorders such as Alzheimer's disease, vascular dementia (from strokes or a lack of blood flow), LBD and the myriad of other diseases under the umbrella of dementia can also cause mental illness. We tend to focus on the cognitive parts of these diseases, but the brain is a complex organ and when it has a disease, this disease can affect many things other than memory. Also, the process of having your brain deteriorate can cause anxiety, depression, and paranoia. How sad and frustrating to know that you cannot remember how to cook a simple meal. How nervous might you get about a family gathering when you cannot remember the names of your grandchildren? And losing things – is there anyone reading this who has not yelled "Who moved my keys?" only to realize that you indeed left your own keys somewhere they don't belong. It's stressful! The disorientation of dementia must feel so frustrating. I am sure it affects people's moods and anxiety levels.

Reassurance, organization, communication, repeated communication, reminders and slowing the pace of activities can help lessen the anxiety, depression and paranoia associated with dementia and other brain diseases. Sometimes medications can be helpful, but those that are used for anxiety and paranoia (or psychosis) come with side effects such as increased fall risk, increased problems with cognition and sleepiness. Using these pharmaceutical tools has to be weighed against the benefit, and managed closely by a healthcare provider. Evaluation and re-evaluation for cognitive and psychiatric medications is important. Don't put your dad on antipsychotics early in his process through dementia, and then never check again to see if they can be tapered off. Committing to pharmaceutical relief should be an active and on-going process to determine if they work, if they cause too many side effects, and if they are still needed. As the brain changes, medications may or may not be necessary anymore. Also, if a patient is prescribed one medication and it doesn't work, it should not be left on the medication regime.

Inappropriate Behaviors

Sometimes I look forward to my older years in which I will feel I can just say whatever is on my mind – loudly and without consequence. One of the families I worked with took their mother to her sister's funeral, as the minister droned on about how wonderful the deceased was, their mother said in a stage whisper "This is horse shit!" A loss of filters and social cues seems to go along with dementia. Maybe it is the cognitive decline, maybe it's chronic pain leading to chronic grumpiness or maybe we just cease to care. It's hard to tell. There is a difference though between the occasional off-color comment, and actions that really impact others or decrease the former dignity of the elder.

One company I have worked with calls inappropriate behaviors, "behavioral expressions." I like this approach to difficult behaviors, because it indicates that getting to the root of a behavior can help us change it. If an elderly lady with dementia frequently disrobes in public, she may simply be hot. An elder who gets up at night and roams in and out of rooms, may simply be hungry or thirsty at night. The keys to helping with inappropriate behaviors are 1) adjusting your own expectations; 2) looking for a reason behind the behavior; 3) finding ways to redirect behaviors; 4) talking with a physician or health care provider, and 5) trying pharmacological treatment if nothing else works.

First, for example, taking an elder out to a family party with lots of activity, noise and people for a long time might be so fatiguing that he lashes out at people. Don't overdo it. Tailor activities, especially public and social activities to the elder's abilities. Although, the aforementioned mother may have previously whispered what she thought of her sister's funeral, she could not hear well anymore causing her to loudly state her opinion. If you didn't know already, people with hearing impairment cannot whisper, because they cannot hear themselves. So, church, weddings, funerals and fancy restaurants may be accompanied by some shouted criticisms or snarky comments that would normally be done quietly.

Especially if an elder has dementia, behaviors may range from the mildly irritating (rummaging through drawers, criticisms, hiding things) to those that put others at risk such as wandering, physical aggression, or sexual aggression. The serious, dangerous behaviors require serious intervention. No matter the reason: hitting, kicking, pushing, or biting others even by people with dementia has to be dealt with quickly and taken seriously. Aggressive behaviors not only cause harm to others, but they also lead to a lack of care for the senior. If an elderly woman with dementia is going to hit her caregivers every time they try to shower her, she won't get showered very often. These behaviors can also lead to discharge from elder care facilities. There are very limited care options for elders with aggressive behaviors.

I recently re-admitted a resident who came back from the hospital and she was hitting the nurses at the hospital. Her family wanted to her to come back to her large low bed for end-of-life care. This large, low bed would require care staff to lean way over her for care and expose themselves even more to being punched, pinched and slapped. So, I asked that they switch her to a hospital bed, both to save the backs of the caregivers and to reduce their exposure to her fists. Small changes like this can help.

Again, try to get to the root of the problem with aggression. Is the person scared? Do they understand what the caregiver is trying to do? Are they too tired? Then try different strategies – if the senior with dementia is afraid of certain caregivers, try others. Try having a family member be present during certain types of care such as showers to help the senior feel more at ease. Explain slowly what is going to be done before care. Minimize intimate care by changing the way it is done. Showers can be given with underwear on. Clothes can be changed in a way that a senior never has to be completely exposed by removing one item at a time, and replacing that item with a clean one. Seniors who want to leave a room or building should just have an escort until they want to go back in, instead of trying to prevent them from leaving. Saying "yes" as often as possible will help decrease frustration and hopefully decrease aggression. Remember that hired caregivers should not be victims of physical or verbal abuse. It is not just "part of the job." They may be accustomed to it because of past experiences and practices, but it is a problem that should not be shrugged off. Decreasing physical aggression is not an easy problem to solve, but no one should give up. The good news is that these issues will go away in the course of dementia, and that there are tools to use that may help.

Second, look for a reason for the behavior so you can try to meet the need before the behavior happens. Is the person agitated because they are in pain? Is your grandfather exit-seeking because he loves to be outside? Is your aunt hitting male staff because she was a victim of sexual assault in her past, and she is now very frightened?

Redirection is a technique that takes advantage of limited memories and short attention spans. It is an attempt to change the situation or mood that diffuses the problem. Knowing the person with dementia-related behaviors will help you find something to capture his anger and attention, and send him in another direction. Some examples are below.

- Your mother is starting to become agitated and yelling that she is trapped and wants to go "home." Try: "Mom, I know you want to go home, but can you help me do these dishes (fold this laundry, set the table, fix this sink…) first? Then, we will go." By the time the task is done, she may forget she wanted to leave.

- Your uncle keeps patting the caregiver's butt while she transfers him to his wheelchair. Try: "Uncle Joe, can you hold this paper for me?" Now he has something to keep his hands busy.

- Your friend is crying because she just got lost in the grocery, and now she is flustered, and won't leave with you. Try: "Hey! Can you tell me about your favorite dinner as a kid?" Talking for a while about a long-term memory will make her feel more comfortable and trigger a feeling that you are friends.

Redirecting can seem really strange at the time, especially if there are other people around trying to have "logical" discussions and convince the elder with dementia of the error of his or her ways. I have gotten many what-in-the-world-are-you-talking-about looks over the years doing this. I promise thought that it works really well.

Another distraction and redirection technique is therapeutic lying. I am a terrible liar and a totally compulsive truth teller. I will blurt out whatever I have done wrong without even being asked. Therefore, I am a very unconvincing liar even when it is a joke or I am trying to do this to soothe an elder with dementia. So, if I can help ease someone's anguish by therapeutic lying so can you. Often therapeutic lying looks like this: Your 90-year-old Aunt Ellen is starting to pace and look out the windows at 5:00 pm. You ask if you can help. Ellen says, "My kids should be back from school by now. It's getting late." Of course, you know that Ellen's kids are 65 and 68 years old now. Also, you know that Ellen believes they are in elementary school. Because you grew up with your aunt and cousin's you know that her kids liked to spend afternoons down the street at a mutual friends when they were growing up. So, you say, "I think they are at your neighbor Jane's house for dinner." This sounds right to Ellen, so she is satisfied and relieved. You may have to repeat this a few times, but soon the crisis will be over and Ellen will move on to other things.

If you cannot prevent a behavior, work on distracting and redirecting a your loved one who is having an inappropriate behavior. If this isn't working, make sure you and others are safe, and not about to lose control. Know your limits and take a break if a behavior is agitating you. Work on making visits and interactions in settings that minimize inappropriate behaviors. Ask for help, an outside perspective might help you understand what is happening.

Also consider if the behavior is truly inappropriate or if it just bothers you.

Recently, a colleague and I were trying to help a 93-year-old resident with Alzheimer's dementia and a bladder infection (a combination that can cause increased confusion and behaviors). This elderly woman was in danger of falling, because of her weakness and agitation so a staff member had to be present with her for hours. At different times, the woman felt that we were bystanders at a car accident, naughty children, her co-workers and I was even a "hussy" who stole her son away. She chewed us out for hours for various infractions. Mostly it didn't bother us much, but in the moments that one of us got frustrated, we took a break and then came back relaxed again.

The formal way of dealing with difficult dementia-related behaviors is to work through a behavior management plan. This is a plan that addresses the triggers for a behavior and the reactions that professional caregivers or family might have to stop the behavior. These should be a working plan in which families and health care workers try different methods until they find something that helps.

So, for example….

Ruby Smith seems to hate getting showers. She refuses to accept a shower on most days, but when she does occasionally accept, she hits and pinches the nurse's aide when she is transferring into a shower. What could be causing that? What can the aides or the family attempt to do to help? Did this tactic work? Did that tactic work? How many times was it tried? Below is an example of how a behavior management plan can be designed.

Behavior Management Plan – Ruby Smith			
Behavior	**What happened prior to behavior?**	**Interventions to try** Change caregivers Provide warm, comforting elements Change the shower time	**Success Partial success/ Failure**
Refusing shower	Breakfast	Approached three times.	Failed
Refusing shower	Breakfast	Brought Ruby a warm towel from the dryer.	Success after 2 attempts
Refusing shower	Assisted out of bed	Brought her a warm towel from the dryer. Changed shower time.	Success

Refusing shower	Assisted out of bed	Brought her a warm towel. Changed shower time.	Success
Hitting shower aide while getting into the shower.	Assisted out of bed	Accepted a shower. Showered at new shower time. Brought warm towel. Provided a calm, quiet atmosphere.	Failed Starting hitting shower aide when she was getting into the shower.
Hitting shower aide while getting into the shower.	Ate breakfast	Accepted shower. Brought warm towel. Provided calm, quiet atmosphere. Asked Ruby to hold a wash cloth	Partial success. Yelled and hit aide with wet washcloths when she got into the shower. Aide started talking to Ruby about the upcoming

		in each hand.	reading activity and she calmed down.
Hitting shower aide.	Assisted out of bed	Accepted shower. Brought warm towel. Provided calm, quiet atmosphere. Asked Ruby to hold a wash cloth in each hand. Chatted about upcoming activities and the weather throughout the shower.	Success. No hitting. Ruby was calm through shower. Chatting and washcloths provided distractions.

Example Behavior Management Plan for Showering

Behavior Management Plan – Ruby Smith			
Behavior	**What happened prior to behavior?**	**Interventions to try** **Assist with eating** **Seat Ruby last** **Seat Ruby first** **Seat Ruby after meal is on the table** **Remind Ruby not to hit her table mates** **Seat caregiver with her at table.**	**Success/ Partial Success / Failure**
Pinching/Hitting table mates	Assisted in wheelchair from her room.	Seated her first.	Failure. Tried to slap at tablemate's arm when she was seated.
Pinching/Hitting table mates	Assisted Ruby in wheelchair from activity room.	Seated her first.	Failure. Tried to slap.

Pinching/H itting table mates	Assisted in wheelchair from her room.	Seated her last.	Partial success. Ruby seemed content until dessert then she pinched tablemate.
Pinching/H itting table mates	Assisted in wheelchair from her room. Seated her last.	Had food on the table when she was seated.	Partial success. Tried to pinch another resident when he reached for his own drink.
Pinching/H itting table mates	Assisted in wheelchair from activity room. Seated last with food on the table.	Used different color placemats and reminded Jane that her placemat is red.	Success. We kept her cup, plate and dessert on her placemat. Ruby did not attempt to pinch or slap tablemates.

Example Behavior Management Plan – Physical Aggression at Meals

In these two examples of behavioral management plans, we can see a possible underlying cause. First, that Ruby wants to be warm and re-assured of warmth for her showers.

Going straight from a warm bed to a warm shower, followed by a warm towel is more attractive for Ruby so she is more likely to agree. In the second example, with a more serious problem of Ruby being aggressive towards other residents (and thus violating their rights to not be hurt), various ideas were used to decrease conflict. Turns out that Ruby was raised with three hungry brothers who tried to get more food than she did, so she is protective of her food. Her vision problems make it difficult for her to really recognize what is hers and what food belongs her table mates. Seating her last decreased the wait time and potential for anxiety about mealtime. Giving her a colored placemat that demarcates her zone for her food helps her see which food is hers and reduces conflict over things like desserts and drinks that are placed between residents.

If a behavior management plan just doesn't stop a problem behavior then you can consider medication. There are many anti-psychotics that might decrease delusional thinking and anti-anxiety medications that might decrease aggression. As discussed in the section on falls, the reason that these are not prescribed frequently is that they come with serious side effects especially falls. Because falls in elderly are dangerous and traumatic, we are wary of anything that might increase that risk. On the other hand, imagine feeling so confused, delusion or angry that you are hitting, kicking or scared of everyone around you. That sounds miserable to me. If a senior didn't live a life like that prior to cognitive changes, imagine how horrible it must feel to have to resort to physical aggression to manage your life and environment. For many people at this stage, anti-psychotics bring relief. Yes, they may live a shorter life, or have an increased fall risk, but the quality may also improve.

Below is an example of attempts at non-medication interventions (non-pharmacological interventions) that can't be controlled, and thus behavior management is referred on to the physician or healthcare provider.

Threatening/Pushing/Attempting to hit another resident – Jose Sanchez			
Behavior – Verbal and physical aggression toward other male resident	What happened before behavior?	Interventions to attempt: Rest Quiet activities Taking resident for a walk Swimming Using calming music Using essential oil diffusers	Success/Partial Success/Failure,
Verbal and physical aggression.	Resident was napping on the couch and woke up. Other resident was	Rest, essential oils on.	Failure. Yelled at other resident to "get out of my house" and got up and

	standing in the doorway of his room.		charged at other resident. Male staff member had to firmly ask resident to stop and reassure him that other male resident wasn't a threat.
Verbal and physical aggressi on	Both had been sleeping. Staff were helping another resident and didn't see him get up.	Swimming during day to help tire him and provide exercise.	Failure. Jose was found in other resident's room with a hair brush raised to hit him. Female staff had to physically intervene. Jose continued to pace and yell afterward. Other resident was angry.

| Verbal and physical aggression | Was in garden. | Walking outside. | Failure. Held door shut to courtyard when another male resident tried to come in from the garden. Staff had to intervene. Jose continued to yell at and threaten other male resident. |
| Verbal and physical aggression | Resting in room. | Resting. Essential oils. | Failure. Jose hit caregiver in face. Referred to physician for possible medications to stop aggressive behaviors. |

Example of Behavior Management Plan – Aggression

Abuse, Neglect, Exploitation

As people grow older, they can be targets of abuse, exploitation and neglect. One in ten older Americans experiences abuse or neglect, and more than half of this is perpetrated by families[xvii]. I wish this was not true. The elderly can be more vulnerable psychologically, cognitively and physically. Elder abuse, neglect and exploitation are too common in our society. Elderly people can be afraid to speak up, because they may lose the support of family members or they may not want to get people into trouble. Although we hear about more abuse in nursing homes and senior living communities, most abuse happens at home. Healthcare workers are at least subject to background checks and oversight while family and some in-home helpers are not.

Neglect is the willful denial of a person's needs (food, hydration, shelter, a clean environment, heating, cooling, lack of personal care.) Exploitation is usually financial in nature – for example, if a niece gets ahold of a credit card belonging to an elderly aunt and pays her own bills, or if a neighbor uses a car without permission. Physical, psychological and sexual abuse happens when a person purposefully hurts an older adult. This can be done out of frustration or it can just happen because the perpetrator has problems of his or her own. Caregivers, both professional and family, can reach the point of burn out where they might push or strike, belittle or threaten an older adult. No matter the reason, there is no excuse for elder abuse. Sexual abuse also happens and this is just something I can't explain. I know it happens, but I really have no way of explaining this. If any type of abuse happens, it has to be reported. Healthcare workers are required to report suspicions of abuse to maintain their licenses due to regulations set forth in the Elder Justice Act[xviii] and other state laws.

If you suspect abuse or neglect of your older loved one, it is best to report it to a state hotline or the police. These are signs to look for:

- Increased fear
- Sudden change in mood
- Withdrawal
- Unexplained bruising
- Change in financial status
- Soiled clothing
- Skin sores especially in places where the person might sit or lie such as on the buttocks, heels, elbows, between the knees indicating lack of movement.

You can report suspicions for abuse or neglect to a healthcare provider such as a family physician or in an emergency room, by calling adult protective services in your state or by notifying the police. There are many avenues to report abuse. It won't stop if we don't report it. As I worked as a leader in eldercare, I tried to teach and reinforce with our staff that we should be happy to have adult protective services in our building to investigate, because we all want the same thing – to protect elders. In the senior living business, there are also many unsubstantiated reports of abuse, neglect and exploitation. Sometimes, bruises from a fall may look suspicious, or refusals of something like showers may lead to the appearance of neglect. I even had a family report the staff for theft – what were our staff stealing? Used bobby pins.

But that was definitely an outlier. All allegations of abuse, neglect and exploitation have to be taken seriously. The process can require time and effort by multiple agencies, family and the elder. So, make sure you have an idea of what has been happening before you report it.

If an elder has signs of abuse, neglect or exploitation or they simply tell you about a situation, please believe them and investigate it, or have someone else investigate. Remember though with cognitive decline, seniors do sometimes become confused and accusatory. For this reason, I suggest you follow the advice of "trust but verify." Our first response should be to take allegations seriously. That doesn't mean you have to fly off the handle, confront possible perpetrators and demand immediate action. It means that accusations should be investigated and the cognitive status, mental health and history of the resident should be considered. Elder abuse is real. We can't t assume that it was a figment of a resident's confused imagination. We have to protect them. Now, did we steal those bobby pins? No. But we did help investigate it, and the family even put cameras in the resident apartment to reassure their mother that the staff were not stealing anything from her. Even if an abuse, neglect or exploitation report turns out to be false, investigations can help sort out any problems and concerns.

If your loved one makes false accusations against you or someone else you know to be innocent consider protecting yourself by not visiting alone, making sure others know where valuables are kept or securing them so they don't get lost, having a co-signer for accounts if you are helping with finances and reporting incidents (like falls) to a healthcare provider so that injuries don't show up unexplained. It is a sad situation to feel like you have to protect yourself from accusations, but in healthcare we do this frequently. Sometimes reality becomes confused with the past, with television and even with dreams as people with cognitive decline age.

Allegations of abuse, neglect and exploitation are public for licensed senior care facilities. State departments of health usually have this information along with a yearly inspection of facilities published on their state websites usually under the category of health or social services.

End-of-Life Care

As much as we know that the end-of-life is coming for all of us, we do tend to put off preparing for it. Even when we see the decline over time, families often still feel unprepared for the actual dying process or death. Maybe it's just part of human nature not to really want to let go of life. I have been through many deaths with seniors and their families. Most have been peaceful at the end, but the days and weeks ahead can be very stressful. Preparing for the end-of-life can help decrease stress and decision making at a very difficult time. Having certain paperwork in order provides guidance for loved ones and medical professionals when a person can no longer advocate for themselves. Clarifying decisions about end-of-life is especially important if there are multiple family members or caregivers involved. For example, if a senior has three sons who have different beliefs and education, end-of-life decisions can cause significant conflict. Without clear decisions, medical professionals generally have to default to aggressive treatment. If a dying person has not made it clear that they do not want CPR, IVs, feeding tubes, or respirators, medical professionals have to do what is best for preserving life.

In the past, I have worked with families who at different times have gotten their mother to designate different children as the power of attorney, then I was faced with multiple copies of decision-making documents. This just makes it hard for anyone to make decisions about care, and can lead to intervention from the courts or Adult Protective Services. If you anticipate family conflict over care, have your elder loved one work with a third party – like an attorney – to clearly designate who can make final decisions over health and finances. Then, with their physician or health care provider (such as a nurse practitioner) complete the end-of-life tools such as "do not resuscitate" or "POLST" forms. These are explained in greater detail below. A "Do Not Resuscitate" order simply requests that CPR is not done. A POLST (Physicians Order for Life Sustaining Treatment) has more detailed information regarding interventions[xix].

Very few people really prepare themselves or their loved ones for end-of-life decisions. Medically, several documents need to be readied to clarify final wishes. Do yourselves, your family and your medical providers a huge favor and complete these together.

Are you a "DNR?" A DNR order means Do Not Resuscitate. Resuscitation is that dramatic event on TV shows or in movies when a patient stops breathing and his heart stops beating. Everyone in scrubs rushes in and pumps his chest, gives him IV drugs and puts a mask with a balloon (a bag-valve mask) over his face and pumps air into his lungs. This is the absolute end of life. This order is valid only if and when your heart stops, and you stop breathing. A DNR order does not mean that the medical team won't treat you for other illnesses, or fix your broken femur. A lot of care goes on before the DNR can be invoked. Some people continue to be concerned that having a DNR order means that they won't receive treatment. This is not true.

A DNR order can be part of a more complex document called a POLST – Physician's Orders for Life Sustaining Treatment. Different states have variations on the POLST and may go by a slightly different name. People often have multiple copies of a POLST, and some put them on the refrigerator for the paramedics to see if they are called to their homes. A POLST includes a DNR order (or a full resuscitation order if you prefer), but it also has other details including. Do you want aggressive treatment before your heart stops? Do you want IVs? Do you want artificial nutrition and hydration? Or, do you want to only have "Comfort Measures." Comfort measures mean that the medical team will treat you only to keep you comfortable. So, you might not get IV antibiotics if you get pneumonia, but they might give you oxygen, or medicine to decrease pain and anxiety. An example of how to use this is that most people on Hospice have a DNR with comfort measures only on their POLST. Both a DNR order and a POLST have to be completed in-person, and a doctor or nurse practitioner has to sign them with you.

Living wills can be longer and can provide information on how you want to be treated if you cannot speak for yourself. They are designed to include who you want to make decisions if you cannot, whether you want a feeding tube, what to do if you are in a coma and for what length of time. A living will is not a doctor's order, and does not have to be signed by a doctor. They do not include a DNR. They are usually quite long and full of legal verbiage making them very difficult to invoke in an emergency. Designating a health care power of attorney (HCPOA) and a financial power of attorney (FPOA) and an alternate is often part of a living will process. An attorney can help you through this process to designate people who can make decisions for a loved one if he or she is incapacitated. Some people chose one person for each role so that decision making is spread around a bit. However, remember that this can cause issues if they do not agree. If the HCPOA wants Mom to have more care and the FPOA doesn't want to authorize the money to pay for that care, decision making can become really complicated. Also, a person, even with limited capacity, can still make decisions for him or herself. HCPOA and FPOA do not supersede an individual's wishes if they are still able to make decisions. Another level of decision-making power is guardianship. This has to be decided by a judge and is a longer and more complicated process for an incapacitated elder or other person who can no longer make decisions. Designating a HCPOA and a FPOA before they are needed is critical because if an elder becomes incapacitated through dementia or some other problem, they can no longer designate a power of attorney and families or loved ones have to go through the guardianship process.

All of these documents can be changed or revoked if the primary person changes his mind about his care, and is alert and able to do this. Just be sure to destroy old copies and tell his loved ones about any changes.

Understanding Types of Elder Care

At some point many seniors need help. Limited mobility, cognitive decline, illness and social isolation commonly create needs for assistance with daily life. From a tiny amount of support to full care, seniors may need a changing and complex plan. As people age and change, the need for care may change. You may think that you will progress from a little help to a lot of help, but this can also be dynamic. Care needs may ebb and flow over time depending on social and physical circumstances. Don't feel locked into a certain amount of care. Re-evaluate as you go and consider changes along the way.

Elders may decide for themselves what they need, or they may need help with decisions. For many people, it is hard to allow someone else to help. Whether the help is coming from a grandchild or a hired professional caregiver, many people struggle to accept assistance. Be patient and go slow if you can, and of course as I have said throughout the first part, communicate about possible current and future needs. If you can communicate early about the preferences of seniors in many different future circumstances, then you will be all the better if and when those needs arise. Someone might say they never want to go in a nursing home, but ask them "what if it is just for a few weeks after surgery?" You might also want to balance a desire to stay at home with loneliness or an inability to stay safe. Know preferences, but leave room for changing circumstances and needs.

Throughout the aging process and the need for care, the more you can integrate help from loved ones the cheaper and more personalized the care will be. If you have a loved one who needs full care, but there are three family members who can take one meal a week to help their loved one eat, those days will be meaningful for the senior and may decrease care costs. Or, if you can help your loved one go on outings that relate to his/her own interests, it will brighten his/her day. Some families chose to help with specific care tasks like laundry or showers. The possibilities are endless. You can almost always match the interests and availability of friends and family with some part of elder care needs.

Caring for someone is a loving task whether that means dedicating your whole life to caring for another, or just making sure that a loved one is in a safe, comfortable place. Don't let other people tell you that what you are doing is right or wrong. Taking care of elders seems to be only second in unsolicited advice to having a baby. Everyone has an opinion, but friends and families just have to do what they can. It won't be helpful to take care of your grandmother at home if you are completely exhausted and financially strapped. You just do your best. Do what you can. Ask for help. And don't feel guilty about what you "should" be doing. Guilt and worry just won't help you be a better caregiver for your loved one. Also, not everyone has a great relationship to their elderly family members and providing care can be a real emotional strain in these situations. It is ok to set limits on what you feel you can or should do.

Family and Friends

I am starting the discussion of care with having a network of family and friends to help. I am not starting with you do everything on your own, because I just don't recommend that. Unless your loved one is super independent and just needs a very small amount of help, you should not go it alone. So, once you have your group of 2 or 20 people who want to help divide up the needs and tasks that can be done, then start planning. The table below is an example of how this might look for a senior who needs help but stays at home.

Concerns – arthritis, isolation, poor nutrition – Donald, Age 79		
Helper	**Task**	**Frequency**
Brett – neighbor	Check-in and bring mail	Monday to Friday
Joshua – nephew	Make lunches and bring them over	Tuesday, Friday, Saturday
Lisa – daughter	Take to senior lunch Grocery shop for snacks and easy meals	Monday, Wednesday
Donna – daughter	Take to doctor's appointments, Review medications with doctor and pharmacist	Once or twice a month
Tom – Hired handyman	Put grab bars in the bathroom and put in a higher toilet and walk-in tub	Once
Kim, Luke and Matthew – grandchildren	Social visits, walks and straighten up house	Sundays

Example of Care Needs at Home

For family and friends helping a senior who lives in a retirement community such as an assisted living or memory care, a task chart may look like this:

Bill, age 83 Concerns: COPD, refusing showers, weight loss, isolation		
Helper	**Task**	**Frequency**
Willow – daughter	Laundry and check cleanliness of his room, buy supplies such as toothpaste, toiletries, incontinence supplies	Weekly
Leyna – grand daughter	Visit, bring favorite treat, share music or a video	Twice a week
Luke – son	Help staff with showers to make Bill feel comfortable getting clean	Three times per week
Lauren – daughter	Meet with facility staff to plan care and discuss changes. Check medications. Attend doctor's visit.	Every 3 months and as needed.
Gina – wife	Visit during lunch and encourage Bill to eat.	Five days per week.
Yoshimi – friend	Fill in for Gina when she needs time away.	A few days per month.
Elizabeth – pastor	Read to Bill. Provide spiritual support.	Once per week.

Example Care Needs in Residential Care

This gives you an idea about how to encourage a lot of people to help with tasks that are doable. This also provides a lot of involvement with the staff of a care facility (memory care in this example.) Involvement in a community like this will really improve communication and care. It is helpful if the group of helpers also communicates with each other on a regular basis so they can share their observations and thoughts. Group e-mails, texts or other electronic communication can help keep everyone informed.

Remember to keep out-of-town loved ones in the loop if you can. If you are that out-of-town loved one try not to blow into town, get frustrated with the state of care and try to change everything. As a nurse, I saw this repeatedly. The son from out of town who visits once a year, sees his mother, gets very upset about her decline, asks why no one has told him how bad she is, demands to see the doctor, nurse, therapists, facility director and creates a lot of bad feelings. The reality is that the in-town loved ones and caregivers don't notice the slow, small changes. They are doing their best to make things right for their loved one and have been communicating with medical and care staff. So, try to loop in out-of-town family and loved ones and if you are the out-of-town loved one, expect to see changes and remember that others are helping on a regular basis. The opposite can also occur. If a senior is primarily cared for by one sibling, for example, when the others try to help, the primary caregiver can get wrapped up in how exactly everything needs to be done. So, if you are the primary caregiver, know that you need help and you will have to let go of some of the details sometimes or others won't be able to do anything. I worked with one family who had cared for their dad at home. He had become too much for them to handle so they moved him into memory care. The daughter, his primary care giver, left several pages of instructions for the staff on the most minute detail including that her dad had to have a half cup of hot cocoa in the morning in his Penn State mug while being in his recliner with his red blanket tucked around his legs and his spittoon at his side. That was just the beginning of the day. Her inflexibility about his care was a recipe for disaster. He did not stay in care, and she did not get the help she needed.

In-Home Care

Bringing care givers into a home to assist with any and all functions of daily living can be very helpful, or it can be a nightmare. It is also the most expensive option for assistance. If your loved one can afford 24-hour care, that's great. At around $30 hour, in home care costs $700 per day. Some in-home care companies give a discount for overnight care. If you can balance in-home care with help from loved ones, that can help decrease costs. Sometimes long-term care insurance or Medicaid can help with the costs of care, but given how inefficient it is (one caregiver to one patient versus one caregiver to 10 or 20 patients), insurers are not very willing to pay for in-home care as an option.

However, there is a balance where in-home care can be worth the cost. If a senior needs 20-30 hours of help per week, it is less than most assisted living communities. Of course this does not account for living costs, meals, or socialization, but these may already be covered in home or with other loved ones. If a senior is safe at home and just needs a few hours per day of assistance, in-home care makes financial sense. That one-on-one care allows for focused assistance and the development of a relationship between a senior and caregiver. Caregivers can tailor care and time to things that a senior enjoys – cooking a meal he or she likes or enjoying a particular book. The attention of the caregiver does not have to be shared among a group of residents.

As in other types of care, make sure when hiring in-home care that you understand what training the caregiver has, what kind of background check the caregiver has, and how much the caregiver is paid. You might also want to ask what happens if your assigned caregiver is sick or on vacation, and what the turnover rate is for caregivers.

If you hire on your own, be careful to do your own background checks. You can call your local or state health and welfare department to ask how to do this where you live. Check training and credentials. Know that you will have to fill in if the caregiver becomes ill. And remember that you are responsible for taxes and social security in addition to the hourly wage.

Finally, check on in-home caregivers sometimes. Make sure your loved one is getting the care they need, and that the caregiver is giving them appropriate attention and help. Make your expectations clear and hold the caregiver accountable. It doesn't make sense to pay someone to play games on their phone while your mother watches TV. Make sure you fully utilize the care you are paying for. Encourage private caregivers to maintain their friendly, but professional focus on your loved one. As much as we might love the private caregiver, he or she is hired to support the elder and the family. Private caregivers need to keep their own struggles (personal life, money, childcare) away from the elder they care for. I know this sounds harsh, but I have seen many families supporting the private caregiver more than the private caregiver supports them. It can create a tangled and stressful situation.

Local Senior Centers and Services

Even the smallest rural communities I have visited have a senior center. It might share space with the library or the fire station, but there is a place to go have a meal and socialize. Larger towns and cities have even more amenities and may provide many different programs for seniors including meals, interest groups (bridge, mahjong, reading, painting), educational classes, exercise classes, outings, and help with technology. Seriously, the list is endless. This summer, I read an activities list from a Denver-area senior center that advertised a theatre trip to go see "The Full Monty" and a rafting trip. (When can I join!?) The best part is – it is mostly free or low cost. Senior centers can provide a lot of support for the day-to-day life of elders whether they are living at home or in a care community. So, encourage, cajole, and push your loved ones to join the group if they can.

Most towns and cities also provide transportation on accessible buses to areas around the community. These usually require making an appointment for your ride 24 hours or more in advance. There are two ways to use this service. First is if a senior wants to go someplace on his/her own and doesn't drive anymore. So, for example, if they want to go to the grocery or to a movie, they can get a ride. The other way is if you cannot get an elder loved one in your car because of mobility problems, but you want to go out with them. Say, for example, you want to take your mother to the zoo, but she is in a wheelchair. The senior ride service can transport your mom in a wheelchair accessible vehicle and you can meet her there. Rides are usually low cost and some places have tokens for seniors who have very limited funds and use state services such as Medicaid.

Adult Day Programs

Adult day programs (also known as adult day care or adult day health) are great additions for families who might be able to take care of an elder in the evenings, but need to work during the day. Services are usually tailored to elders who are not safe at home alone. Adult day care facilities provide meals, activities and a place to nap during the day. Adult day health services usually include assistance with toileting, hygiene and some even provide showering help as this can be a very difficult task at home. The cost may be covered by insurance, Medicare or Medicaid or it might be private pay. Adult day care can also be used as a respite for caregivers who are on 24-7 providing care at home or provide another outlet for stimulation if an elder is struggling in a small, long-term care or assisted living community with limited activities or outings.

Residential Care

Helping a loved one navigate choices in elder residential care perplexes even the best planners. Long-term care jargon can be difficult to understand. Is this a nursing home or senior living? Can my mother live in assisted living if she has memory problems? Who decides what is the appropriate place for people? Lines between types of residential care are blurry. There is no strict rule book about who lives where and the types of care offered by different companies and organizations. One company might say that needing help with toileting means that your loved one has to live in a nursing home, while another may offer that assistance in assisted living. Many companies are trying to capture the dollars available for helping seniors so services are quite variable across different companies and facilities. Nursing homes are regulated by both federal and state guidelines, but assisted living and memory cares are only regulated by state codes. So, there is a lot of variation.

The underlying philosophy for all these types of care is that residents should do as much for themselves as possible. You want care that promotes as much independence and self-care as possible so that your loved one does not decline further from lack of use of either brain power or muscles. All residential care is pushing the limit on the number of staff per resident. Facilities may meet state guidelines and therefore be able to say they are not understaffed, but this is because guidelines are so lax. Staff, especially caregivers, nursing assistants and nurses are caring for so many people that they end up rushing and cutting corners. So, if you are looking for a lady's maid and butler, senior living is not the place to go. Think of senior care more like a cross between a favorite aunt and a drill sergeant, they should be kind to your loved one, but they should also push to get them to do as much as they can for themselves.

Senior living is also designed to be as efficient as possible, which means your loved one will share help with many other people. This ratio may be one caregiver for ten people with dementia or one caregiver to thirty people who are in assisted living. This means that if your loved one can only expect 1/10 or even 1/30 of the attention of a caregiver. There will be other support people in the mix such as activities directors and cooks, but the ratio of caregiving staff to residents is for the most efficient care of the elderly, not the most social or most loving, slow or warm care. The many places I have worked and consulted, I know that most employees in senior care have good hearts and want to help people, but they are always limited by their task lists and need to get the basics done. This model not only keeps costs down (and profits up), it is often also very difficult to keep workers in senior care. It is an entry level job with relatively low pay, and it is hard work. Very few people stay in the field for a long time. With attention and oversight, these situations can turn out for the best for your mother or grandfather. However, these are the realities of all elder care that you have to keep in mind while you are considering placement for your loved one. I know a lot of loving and effective care can be provided, but I am not going to pretend it isn't a strain or that every resident is given as much time as they need.

Review of Basic (ADL) and Complex (IADL) Needs

For simplicity, I am going to focus on two key areas to determine the level of care needed. These include: (1) the senior's abilities, and (2) the organizations' services. Costs won't be directly addressed here, but in general, higher levels of care have higher costs.

First, determine how your loved one performs complex (IADL) and basic (ADL) tasks. We discussed this in earlier sections, but I think it is worth a quick review with the perspective of how it relates to care levels. The long-term care industry and the Center for Medicaid and Medicare Services[xx] have a list to consider. Complex tasks are called Instrumental Activities of Daily Living (IADLs) and basic, personal tasks are Activities of Daily Living (ADLs). For the most part, complex tasks are required to stay connected to community. Basic tasks are required to maintain one's own body. The exception is that medication management is considered a complex task or IADL for these purposes.

Complex Tasks (IADLs)	Basic Tasks (ADLs)
Manage finances	Feeding
Transportation (driving or public transit)	Toileting
	Choosing appropriate clothes
Shopping	Grooming
Preparing meals	Dressing
Using phone/communication devices	Undressing
	Bathing
	Walking (ambulating)
Medication management	Transferring from chair or bed
Housework	

Independent Living

Organizations that offer Independent Living or Senior Housing usually help people who have difficulties with complex tasks (IADLs). They also promote more socialization and activity than some elders get at home, or in the homes of family members. In addition, independent living is designed for accessibility and safety – so no more basement stairs to the laundry room or shoveling snow. Also, independent living facilities usually provide an emergency call system that helps your loved one summon a staff member in an emergency. Many independent living senior communities offer cottages or some other kind of detached homes that surround a central building with apartments, other levels of care, dining and activities. These cottages are similar to detached condominiums and can either be rented or bought. Many independent living communities offer weekly housekeeping in cottages or apartments. Meal programs differ from one meal per day to a buy in program that allows independent residents to purchase a number of meals per month. Meals are an easy way to increase socialization in senior communities, even if the resident does not have a lot of needs, sharing a meal with others can help them integrate into the community and learn about other activities. Many places that offer independent living also offer a continuum of care. So, integrating into independent living early may allow a senior to accept higher levels of help in the same campus of buildings when and if they need it. In my experience, these multi-level facilities can also create a clique mindset where independent seniors don't want to associate with people in other levels of care and become very resistant to moving to higher levels of care and becoming one of "those people." So continuing care systems can be both convenient and off-putting depending on the community.

Assisted Living

Assisted living is the next higher level of care. Although I have to once again offer the caveat that there is variability, generally, assisted living provides help with all complex tasks and some basic tasks. Increasingly, assisted living facilities provide help with nearly all personal care. Be sure to ask assisted living organizations for their disclosure of services – a list that tells you what is available if needed. Assisted living facilities are staffed by an oversight nurse (not 24 hour per day nursing), and unlicensed or on-the-job trained care givers.

In assisted living, residents have their own apartment or may share an apartment with one other person. These apartments can be studios, one or two bedrooms. Apartments usually have a refrigerator, sink, microwave and bathroom with shower. To be able to live in assisted living, a senior must be safe on his/her own for several hours at a time, and be able to ask for assistance when needed. For this level of care, a resident must be able to advocate for him or herself. To me this is absolutely the defining line for assisted living versus a higher level of care: Can (and will) your loved one tell the staff when he or she needs help or want something? Put simply, can he advocate for himself?

If for example, Ed is a resident in a one-bedroom apartment in assisted living. Let's say he has developed a cold and just feels weak today. Ed doesn't need help every morning so staff did not come in and see him between 6:00 am and 8:00 am. Now it is 8:30 am and Ed is too tired to go down to the dining room for breakfast. To be appropriate for assisted living, Ed has to be able and willing to summon help with a call light or button, tell someone he isn't feeling well and ask for breakfast to be brought to him. Ed has to be able to advocate for himself.

Now, a good assisted living will check on residents at each meal and make sure they have eaten and are ok, but it is not a fool proof system and depending on how active or able a resident is, staff may have an expectation that a resident will let them know what is needed.

Assisted living facilities follow care plans. So, unless Ed, in our example above, has a care plan that says he has to be escorted to meals or that he needs someone to check on him every two hours. Care staff won't necessarily know to check on him.

Since assisted living is the lowest level of residential care in terms of acuity (or the level of illness and need of the resident), there are fewer safeguards for things falling through the cracks. So, to be appropriate and successful in assisted living, a resident needs to be able to say "hey! I've fallen through the cracks, and I need help."

Willingness can also be a big part of this. If your mother is unwilling to ask for help, then it is really hard for her to be successful in assisted living. Sometimes if your loved one is resentful about being placed in assisted living, they are very willing to suffer and then let you know (or everyone know) how terrible it is. I have been yelled at many times by family members who storm into my office and say, "My mother didn't get dinner!" And I say, "Did she pull her call light to let us know?" Then we figure out that mother often just has cheese and crackers in her room for dinner, tonight, she didn't want that, didn't come down to the dining room, and didn't call anyone for help – except her son (who she really thinks should be taking care of her at home.) So, your loved one has to be able AND willing to advocate for herself to live in assisted living.

Costs in assisted living are split into (1) room and board, and (2) care. Room is the cost of the apartment and utilities, so this will vary by the size and desirability of the apartment. Desirability might be based on location (first floor, distance from activities) or other amenities like windows, view or layout. Board is the cost of meals, housekeeping, maintenance and activities. Care is calculated based on an assessment of needs by a nurse or another licensed person such as a social worker. Some states do allow unlicensed employees to conduct an assessment. There are a few people who have the ability to do this – people with a great deal of experience and who have an ethical heart. However, I would ask for a nurse to conduct any assessment for admission to assisted living. Nurses are trained to understand disease processes, medications, and abilities to safely complete activities of daily living. Nurses also have much less focus on a facility's sales and capacity filling needs. Nurses will put the potential resident first and know the abilities of the care staff in his/her facility. Some assisted livings use a levels model meaning that a resident might be considered a low, moderate or high level of care. Each level is then assigned a financial charge for that level. Other assisted livings charge by detailed lists of care needs.

Example of Detailed Costs for Care			
Care Category	**Levels**	**Cost per month**	**Narrative Example**
Mobility	Independent	$0	Resident can walk safely to meals and activities with cane.
	Needs direction and assistance with finding way	$90	Resident needs help finding the dining room for meals and the activity room for reading and exercise.
	Needs one person to escort for safety	$300	Resident walks with a front-wheel walker and needs one person assist to walk with her for safety and to stop and rest when needed
	Needs wheelchair pushed	$390	Resident uses a wheelchair for mobility. Needs staff member to push wheelchair long distances outside his room.

Bathing	Independent	$0	Resident showers himself daily. Uses a shower chair.
	Needs reminders and set up.	$90	Resident is forgetful about showering. Needs care staff to remind him to shower and to set out shampoo, towel and change of clothes.
	Needs set up and hands-on assistance for showers.	$300	Resident will shower twice a week. She needs help washing her lower legs and feet, and shampooing her hair. She will use a shower chair. Likes to shower in the evenings.

	Needs hands-on assistance for bath in the Jacuzzi.	$600	Resident likes to bathe. Requires care giver to take to Jacuzzi spa, bring shampoo, soap, warm towel and change of clothes. Assist into bath, adjust water, fill tub, assist to wash her back. Care staff must stay in spa room for safety during bath.

Memory Care

Memory care is a subset of assisted living that provides more behavioral interventions, directed activities geared to those with cognitive impairment, a quieter environment, and most personal care or ADLs. Memory care can be a stand-alone facility, or be part of another assisted living. These memory care facilities usually have staff that has additional training in dementia, but staff members are not necessarily licensed as nurse's assistants or nurses. These areas have the same type of nurse oversight model as other assisted livings, but the emphasis is usually more on the structure of activities than medical aspects of care. If your loved one has any of the following difficulties, consider a memory care facility.

Gets lost around the house or yard

Repeatedly tries to leave or leaves house unattended

Becomes agitated when confused

Hits

Yells and screams

Sexually aggressive or inappropriate behaviors

Cannot tell people what he or she needs

Cues, such as reminders or notes, don't improve abilities

Becomes very agitated in group settings such as dining rooms

Falls frequently when alone

Cues That Memory Care Is Needed

A good memory care can be beneficial to someone with dementia. The additional staffing, specially designed programming and atmosphere can create less stress and provide more comfort for people with dementia. Although it can feel difficult to move a loved one into a locked specialized dementia care facility, it can bring relief. An important note is that dementia care units are locked. Be prepared for this feature. Being locked in to a care facility can be an emotionally difficult hurdle for both residents and their loved ones. A well-designed memory care will disguise the locked aspect of the facility by providing diversions to the exit door. Look for a memory care that incorporates design, programming and clinical oversight to provide the best experience. All memory care facilities should have extensive social and recreational programming.

Memory care programming should include multiple sensory activities. Look for the following features in a memory care.

Touch/Tactile – There should be tactile activities including different materials that a resident can touch and hold. This might include a touch table with for example shells and sand. Soft materials including fleece or fuzzy blankets for comfort. Weighted blankets that help with anxiety. Busy blankets with snaps, buckles, pockets, and velcro for busy hands. Rocking chairs or gliders that go side-to-side to soothe restlessness and anxiety. Weighted dolls for holding and comfort. Dolls designed for people dementia have been developed to provide the weight and feel of a baby. They can even be scented to smell like baby powder. Men and women who have raised or just love children can feel very comforted and purposeful holding these babies. Sometimes, people with dementia know the babies are dolls and sometimes they don't, so be careful how you handle them. (Once, I set one of these on a dining table while helping a resident, and it caused a lot of outrage. I never did that again!)

Smell – Aromatherapy can help with waking, calming and sleeping. Different scents should be used throughout the day to signal different activities and moods in the memory care community. In addition, activities such as baking can help stimulated appetites for residents in memory care. Although it can be difficult to manage the smell of multiple incontinent residents, memory care should not smell like urine or feces frequently.

Sight – Dementia care areas should feel homelike. Some communities decorate based on past eras that might feel more comfortable for people with dementia. There should be areas that draw attention to activities that might have happened in the past or at home. These include a wood shop type area, a sewing or laundry area, an office area for resident use and other creative ideas. When I worked in a dedicated dementia unit, we didn't have a lot of amenities, but I had a lot of fabric scraps and we spent many afternoons sorting fabric and deciding what would go together for a quilt. We never did make that quilt, but rummaging through fabric was a favorite afternoon activity. Activities that are more designed for traditional male interests are notoriously lacking in memory care. The combination of having a larger female elderly population and a larger number of female caregivers means that men's interests sometimes get a little neglected. Of course, not all women want to sort fabric and not all men want to putter around in the wood shop, but making sure there are a diversity of activities can be important for everyone.

Taste – With dementia comes changes in taste for many people. These changes take various forms including a lack of appetite, a need for more flavorful choices, difficulties in holding and managing food and even constant eating. Dementia care facilities should offer a liberalized diet meaning that there are not strict rules about what someone can or cannot eat. Residents in dementia care still have the right to choose and the right to refuse food. Staff in memory care facilities should encourage eating a variety of foods, but they cannot force your father to eat his vegetables and not eat dessert.

In addition to differences in taste, diseases such as Alzheimer's dull the ability to see making differentiating between a meal that includes chicken, corn and potatoes on a white plate impossible. Memory care should provide different colors of food on a contrasting plate. Many communities use red plates as this is supposed to stimulate the appetite and provides a contrasting background to many foods.

Memory cares should also provide easy to eat foods such as sandwiches and vegetable sticks to make it easier to pick up and eat. This is especially true for people with a limited attention span or restlessness. If a resident cannot sit through a meal, then they should be offered a sandwich or some other mobile food to eat while they roam.

Alzheimer's and aging in general can decrease the ability to taste foods. This means that sometimes people in memory care will create what we lovingly called "dementia fusion cuisine" in one community where I worked. It may seem really gross to you, but if your father wants to put his pudding on his meatloaf and eat it that way, then everyone needs to let him.

Water and snacks should always be available in both memory care and other types of senior living communities. Hydration helps with so many different health issues, it should be constantly encouraged and available.

Sound – Music holds a special place in memory care. The parts of the brain that remember and enjoy music are less affected by Alzheimer's and other dementias. Singing familiar songs can really engage people with dementia. There are even choirs made up of people with dementia[xxi]. I worked with a lady with Alzheimer's who was very advanced. She usually just said "HEY! HEY!" over and over if we were not very close to her. But she loved to sing and remembered every word of the old drinking song:

"Show me the way to go home.
I'm tired and I want to go to bed.
I had a little drink about an hour ago,
And it went right to my head..."

Afterwards she would always laugh, and that is a far cry from saying "HEY! HEY!" over and over because you feel alone.

People who may be unable to reach for the right words can often still sing. This makes people really feel a sense of capability when so many other things are difficult. In addition, listening to music and stories can have a soothing and engaging impact on people with dementia. When considering a memory care facility, make sure they understand and use the power of music. They should be able to tailor music to your loved one through individual systems such as iPods or other systems with headphones. Listening to stories, movies and music through head phones or ear buds is very effective for people with dementia. It cuts through all the extraneous noise and distractions and helps them focus. In addition, there are usually musicians who are willing to come play in memory care facilities. A memory care facility should know how to work with local musicians, individual programming and singing activities to enhance the lives of their residents. This can be one of the most powerful ways of reaching someone with dementia.

So, with the emphasis on comfort through design and activities, memory care can be a good choice for someone struggling to engage at home or in another type of senior care. Look for high quality programs, good design and nursing oversight.

Nursing Homes

What most people call "nursing homes" the senior living industry and Medicare call skilled nursing. Skilled nursing facilities (SNFs – pronounced "sniffs") provide help with all basic tasks and complex tasks. They also provide 24-hour a day licensed nurses in the facility with physician oversight, and can complete medical treatments such as IV therapy, mechanical ventilation, tube feeding or wound care. SNFs also provide rehabilitation after an injury or severe illness including intensive physical, occupational and speech therapy. SNFs are the only long-term care option that can accept payment from Medicare. However, this is limited to rehabilitation services. Skilled nursing facilities are staffed by on-site licensed nurses and certified nursing assistants. They also have physician oversight. This type of staffing really raises the bar on clinical oversight in comparison to memory care and assisted living which use limited nursing and on-the-job-trained care staff.

SNFs have a more hospital-like quality including hospital beds, therapy equipment and hospital-like rooms with open doors to the main hallways. SNFs employ nurses to provide care to all residents with the help of CNA's or certified nursing assistants. CNAs provide most of the personal care, and nurses provide oversight, treatments (like bandage changes) and sometimes medication administration. In addition, SNFs have their own social workers and therapy staff. In the past, residents could live in nursing homes for years. Occasionally, this is still the case if a resident wants to pay out of pocket or if they have Medicaid and cannot be helped someplace else, however most residents are there for about six weeks before they are moved to assisted living or home. Elders who go into the hospital due to illness or for a procedure such as a hip replacement are often discharged to SNFs so they can get intensive rehabilitation.

SNFs are required to also have activities, encourage nutrition and hydration, and provide support to residents and families. SNFs should be designed in ways that promote health and social interaction along with physical rehabilitation. Many SNFs were designed and built decades ago and are having difficulty meeting today's aesthetic standards. Look for SNFs that balance medical care with social activities, daylight, available outside areas and healing environments that provide comforting sights, sounds, and smells.

Residents are discharged from SNFs if they are not meeting or have already met their therapy goals. This means that either a senior has recovered and is at baseline (meaning generally back to their pre-illness or pre-surgery abilities), or they cannot make more progress because they either won't participate in therapy or the damage to their body is such that they cannot continue to improve. The social worker should work closely with the resident and his or her family to plan for discharge either to a lower level of care such as assisted living or home.

Changes in Placement Levels

When we look at the different types of care, we need to keep in mind the pressure on the US healthcare system to provide the least expensive, and thus lowest level of care acceptable. In the past, a patient might have spent 10 days in the hospital after a hip replacement and they could receive therapy services there. Now, a patient might be discharged to a SNF instead of convalescing at the hospital. Further, instead of staying in a "nursing home" once a resident no longer needs treatment from a licensed nurse everyday, they are encouraged to move to assisted living or home. In my opinion, acuity creep or the increasing care needs of residents in each level of care can be a real danger for the elderly. Not having 24 hour licensed nursing staff means that someone who may be fairly fresh from a major surgery or illness can quickly become sicker, and it will take longer for the assisted living caregiving staff or in-home caregivers to notice and alert a physician. On the other hand, allowing elders to live in the least restrictive environment means that they might have a higher day-to-day quality of life in their own apartment or house instead of staying in a medically-focused nursing home. The challenge of acuity creep is something that SNFs, assisted living and in-home care agencies are having a hard time meeting. Requirements for front-line staff are not increasing while residents and patients are sicker and sicker. So, this is the changing situation that most patients and health care workers are facing when they are considering placement in different levels of residential care.

In addition to the four main categories of independent living, assisted living, memory care and skilled nursing facilities, there are some less common, but viable, options for elder care. "Swing beds" are long-term care rooms in hospitals. These areas of a hospital are used either to increase the number of patients providing revenue to the hospital, or to mitigate costs if the hospital cannot find placement for a person in need of long-term care. A few factors may contribute to difficulty finding appropriate placement including:

- Inability to pay;
- Dementia-related behaviors;
- Psychiatric illnesses;
- Morbid obesity;
- Resistance to care;
- Drug resistant infections; and
- On-going alcohol and drug abuse.

Group family homes are very small assisted living homes where unlicensed or on-the-job-trained caregivers provide assistance for a few residents – usually less than seven. Nurses provide consulting oversight, and are usually not at the home every day. Sometimes these facilities have live-in care providers, and they are often located in residential neighborhoods.

Adult day programs, as mentioned before, provide a place for elders to go for all or part of the workday to allow family members to continue to work, or to increase socialization, encourage interesting daily activities, and provide respite from difficulties of care. Some are geared toward dementia care others may have a wider variety of clients including people with developmental delays. These centers can take funding from either Medicare, Medicaid or private pay.

As you navigate care options for your loved one, remember to look at what family or friends can do to provide assistance. You may not be able to provide all the care your loved one needs, but if you can choose to assist with one or two of his/her needs this will decrease costs, increase personalization of care, and give you a specific manageable way to help. For example, can you set up medications and provide reminders every day, or set out appropriate clothes for the day?

Further, private caregiving, although costly per hour, can be used to provide small amounts of care and help your loved one stay in a lower level of care that will be less expensive. For example, assisting two or three times a week with bathing may help an elder stay in independent living while increasing their well-being and safety. Afternoon activities assistance with private caregivers may decrease dementia-related behaviors and allow an elder to stay in assisted living instead of moving to a dementia-care facility.

To begin the process of helping a loved one chose the best level of care, honestly assess what they can do and what help you can provide. Ask direct questions to organizations regarding the care they provide and how the care affects costs. When considering any residential care facility to help with your elderly loved one it is important to ask a lot of questions. Below are tables with categories of questions and what you might expect to hear in response. Don't be afraid to ask lots of questions. Most facilities are eager to fill their rooms and gain the income from residents, and they will be very willing to answer questions. Questions and answers you want to anticipate are listed in the tables below. These questions are also available on the worksheet pages at the end of this book and on my website www.juliaparkerconsulting.com.

Questions: Care and services provided

Questions	Expectations
What care do you provide?	Care facilities should have a care disclosure list. These will outline all care provided and care not provided. For example, an assisted living may exclude IV therapy, ventilators, bed bound residents etc. Or a skilled nursing facility may exclude residents with aggressive behaviors.
How do residents request help?	Care facilities should have some type of call system. Preferably, residents should have both a call cord to pull from their bed and bathroom AND have a wearable call button that can be pushed if the call cord cannot be reached. Some facilities have lights that come on outside a resident room in addition to a call board at the nurse's station, others

	have pagers or other electronic systems.
What is the average wait for a call light during each shift?	Most care facilities have a computerized system that lists call lights and time for response. Smaller or older facilities may not have this system, but should check call light time manually at regular intervals. Expect around five to fifteen minute response times. Longer than fifteen minutes should be a red flag.
What kinds of behaviors are you used to dealing with in residents with dementia?	All levels of care work with residents with dementia, these communities should let you know what their limits might be in terms of dementia-related behaviors.
Can you provide transportation?	Many facilities have their own wheel chair accessible vans and buses. If there is no facility van, they should be able to arrange transportation through community services. Depending on the company, the level of income and the

	desired type of transportation (to a doctor's appointment vs. a trip to the store) costs for community-based transportation will differ.
Can I see an activity calendar?	Activities ideally vary and include: social, physical, spiritual and cognitive stimuli. Look through the activities with your loved one to see if there are things she/he would want to do. While at the facility, you might want to check the calendar against what is actually happening. If baking is listed at 2:00 that day and no one is baking, ask why.
Can I see a monthly menu?	Elder care facilities have to plan out nutritious menus. For buildings owned by larger companies, these are planned by dietitians, and there is usually a rotation of foods over a month or a season. Options should be available if the main dish is not preferred by residents. These items are usually called "always available" items and can be things like a grilled cheese, ham and

	cheese sandwich, burgers or other simple options. You and your loved one should be invited to a meal to experience the dining services.
Can you accommodate special diets?	Many elders require special diets such as low sodium, carbohydrate-controlled or soft textures. Ask if these are available. Other requirements or preferences are less common. So, if your loved one needs a vegetarian diet or has allergies or intolerances to certain foods, ask how those can be accommodated.
Can residents eat meals in their rooms? Does it cost more?	Some elder care communities require that residents come to the dining room for meals except in rare circumstances like when they have a cold. Residents usually benefit from coming to meals because they get more social interaction and are visible to multiple staff members during these times. If a resident wants to eat some or all of their meals in their

	room, then a fee is usually added to their care bill. In addition, limited menus might be available for delivery, meals are often served with disposable dishes and plasticware. These are less appetizing than a nice plate and table setting.

Questions: Cost calculations

Question	Expectation
How do you calculate care costs?	Care costs should be transparent. These costs can be calculated by specific need as outlined in previous table on care plans and costs or they can be calculated by high, moderate or low care. Depending on the state, care plans are reviewed every 3 to 12 months and as needed. A nurse or qualified care giver should evaluate care needs regularly.
Is the cost for care in addition to the rent for the room?	Rent for a room is separate from care costs in assisted living. In skilled nursing and dementia care this may be calculated differently.
Can I have the preliminary care costs before we move in?	If this is not an "emergency" admission, care costs should be available prior to move in.

	Occasionally, a hospital ER physician will push for an admission to a care facility in a matter of hours because an elder just is not safe at home. If this is the case, a rough estimate of care costs may be all that is available for the first few days. Otherwise, you should have a good estimate of care costs.
Do they take any insurance?	There are a few types of insurances that may be helpful for care. There are more details about paying for costs later, but check on these: Medicare (Generally only accepted by SNF for rehabilitation.) Long-term care insurance (Can be used for reimbursement for care costs and varies greatly). Medicaid (Can be used in all types of care if a senior is without other means or assets, not all facilities accept residents on Medicaid.)
What happens if we run out of money and have to use Medicaid?	If a resident is living in senior care and has to transition from private pay to Medicaid payments, they may have to move to a facility that takes Medicaid. If you anticipate this issue in the future, ask what might happen.

Questions: Outside Services

Question	Expectation
Do you use a specific pharmacy?	Using one pharmacy that packages drugs in a way that is conducive to giving medications to dozens of people, is efficient for care facilities. In addition, these long-term care pharmacies such as Omnicare or CVS, may be directly connected to the electronic medical record systems and provide pharmacy consulting services. So, many facilities strongly encourage residents to use their preferred pharmacy. However, this means a senior won't be using a pharmacy that they may feel loyal to, and it may not be the cheapest option.
Do I have to use your pharmacy? Is there an extra charge if we don't?	Usually residents are not required to use a certain pharmacy, but it is more efficient, and therefore incentivized. A monthly charge of up to hundreds of dollars may be added to care for residents who do not use the facility's pharmacy.
If applicable, can we use VA?	Most facilities will provide an exception for VA medications. Remember though that the VA is slow to provide medications when needed and you may need to use the facility pharmacy as a backup if

	you need something quickly such as an antibiotic.
Do you have a health care provider who comes in to see residents?	One of the easiest ways to have a senior see a healthcare provider (usually a nurse practitioner) is to sign up with a provider who comes to the facility. In larger cities, there are groups of in-home elder care providers that service assisted living and memory care facilities. SNFs have physician oversight and sometimes also have other providers that visit.
Do you have physical therapy, occupational therapy or speech therapy?	SNFs have in-house therapy, but assisted living and memory care are not required to have this. There are often preferred visiting therapy companies that work with assisted living and memory cares. Some larger senior living companies may have their own therapy services.
Do you work with an outside Hospice provider?	Hospice providers come to senior living facilities to assist with end-of-life care. These are usually outside providers who come to a variety of facilities and homes.

Questions: Staffing

Do you have licensed nurses in the building? How many hours/day?	Depending on the number of residents and the type of care provided nursing hours may range from a few per week to multiple nurses 24-hours per day. When comparing facilities and types of care, use nursing hours as a measure of how they are meeting the care needs of residents.
What kind of training do your care staff get?	SNFs use certified nursing assistants (CNAs) for personal care and nurses (either LPN or RN) for management of medication, assessing health and providing procedures such as wound care. CNA's take a 6-12 week course and pass a licensing exam. Assisted living facilities vary in training based on the management of the building and state regulations. Most assisted living and memory care facilities provide computer based classes and some hands-on training. There are very minimal requirements for training to work in assisted living and dementia care in most states. Also, in assisted living and memory care non-licensed staff give medications, and no standard is in

	place for required training across communities and states. Specialized dementia training should be part of training for any staff member in senior living. These skills can be used to assist seniors with any level of dementia.
What is your care staff to resident ratio?	Care facilities have many staff members including maintenance workers, activity leaders, housekeepers, cooks, dining staff, and business management. However what you really want to know is how many residents per caregiver in the facility or in the part of the facility where your loved one will be living. You will find that care staff to resident ratios are fairly low. Skilled nursing ratios can be 1:10-1:15. Memory care facilities can be 1:6 to 1:15. Assisted living ratios can be 1:15 to 1:30.
What is your care staff to resident ratio for each shift?	The caregiver-to-resident ratio changes throughout the day with day shift being the busiest. Evening shift ratios are lower and night shift is the lowest. I don't recommend facilities that ever have less than two caretakers in the facility at a time no matter how small the facility. If there is an emergency or a fall, it's

	important to have two people to manage the emergency along with other resident needs.
How many hours per day do staff work?	The trend toward 12 hour shifts continues to grow in health care. Most hospitals have 12 hours shifts for nurses and CNAs. Many other residential settings use 12 hour shifts. In addition, due to the shortage of nurses and other healthcare workers, double shifts (16 hours) and overtime are used abundantly. Consider what you feel comfortable with for working hours. Burn out can occur rapidly with long days and lots of overtime.
What do you pay your care staff?	If you don't feel comfortable asking about wages, consider asking if workers make a living wage. A living wage (about $15/hour and up) reduces turnover and attracts more experienced workers. Understanding how much employees are being paid and how much they are asked to work, will help you understand the type of care you might expect.
What is your turnover rate for staff?	I have seen caretaker turnover rates as high as 400% (meaning basically a new staff every 3 months) and as low as 90%. Because of the entry-level work

	and the low wages, be ready for frequent staff turnover. Look for a facility closer to 90% than 400%. Management turnover is high for many senior living companies and nursing shortages can impact rapid turnover of clinical staff.

Questions: Environment and Safety

Question	Expectations
Can I see your last state survey?	The answer to this should always be yes. State surveyors require this information to be available for review.
Is this a locked facility?	Many facilities have locked egress in some way. Doors can never be completely locked because of fire hazards, but they may have a delay, or alarm when people try to exit. Some doors have codes so that residents who are cognitively able can use the code to exit the building while those who need supervision cannot usually manage the code.
Is there an outside area to walk safely?	All facilities should have an outdoor area that is safe for walking or sitting in the fresh air for a bit. The best are courtyards that anyone can use

	no matter what their cognitive status.
Do residents have their own bathrooms?	Some facilities have separate rooms with shared bathrooms, others have en suite bathrooms.
Do residents have their own showers?	In addition, some areas have personal bathrooms, but shared shower areas.
Can residents keep their doors open?	Many assisted living communities discourage leaving apartment or personal doors open. Sometimes this is just an aesthetic choice, but often these are fire doors that have to stay closed. Residents who feel isolated in a room by himself or herself may not like this feature of assisted living.
Can residents adjust the heat in their own rooms?	If your loved ones likes the heat and air conditioning set at a particular level it's important to know if setting the level in each room is available.
Will my loved one have to share a room or apartment?	Sharing rooms is more common in SNFs than in assisted living or memory care. If your loved one is expected to share a room find out how room mates are assigned and what happens if they do not get along. Also, residents on

	medicaid are more often assigned to shared rooms because of the lower reimbursement rates from medicaid. So, it's good to know that if you have to transition to medicaid, you know that your loved one will then have to share a room or apartment.

A Few Additional Options

A few lesser known options for care include the Veteran's Administration, geriatric psychiatric facilities, and respite care options.

The Veteran's Administration (VA) provides care in a skilled nursing facility or nursing home-type care for veterans and their spouses. VA's are often equipped to deal with some of the increased unique needs of veterans including physical and psychological injuries from combat. The VA can also help pay for care in other facilities mentioned in this book. Reach out to a VA service center and apply for benefits for former service members[xxii]. The VA does not move quickly, but they do provide great support.

Geriatric psychiatric facilities (the name is usually shortened to geri-psych because it is a lot easier to say) provide short or long-term care to the elderly with psychiatric conditions that do not allow them to stay safely and comfortably in other types of residential care. Sometimes if a skilled nursing facility or assisted living cannot manage difficult dementia-related behavior or psychiatric conditions, they will recommend a geri-psych facility for placement. Assisted living, memory care and skilled nursing must first show that they have attempted many non-pharmacological and pharmacological interventions to enable appropriate care before requesting a discharge to geri-psych.

Finally, many of the care settings mentioned can provide respite care. If your loved one is at home with family or friends assisting and there needs to be a break in that care, you can ask senior care facilities for a short stay or respite care. These stays usually range from 2-4 weeks. Respite stays can either provide a break for the main caregivers at home or provide a try-out period for a care facility.

Hospice

Hospice provides in-home or in-facility care. Hospice is designed to come to the patient although there are also optional Hospice houses if end-of-life care cannot be done in place. The majority of Hospice care is directed and provided by nurses. A hospice doctor oversees medication and care, but you may rarely see this doctor. Hospice can also coordinate with a primary care doctor if you prefer to use someone else. They work behind the scenes directing care based on the assessments of nurses. Hospice nurses work as case managers and provide hands-on care. If an elder is admitted to Hospice with months ahead of him. Then a Hospice nurse may come see him only once per week, and an aide may come in twice a week to help him bathe. The doctor, nurse, family and patient coordinate what medications may be needed for comfort. Hospice has nurses on-call 24 hours per day and can coordinate with physicians any time day or night to help change medications and make decisions about care. Hospice also has social workers, chaplains, bereavement specialists and volunteers that help. In addition, hospice often orders equipment that might make end-of-life care easier such as a hospital bed or oxygen supplies. However, hospice workers do not provide 24-hour care in the home. At least until near the final days and hours, they don't provide daily care or sit at the bedside at home. If you want that kind of help, you will have to negotiate assistance from loved ones, and perhaps add paying for private-duty nurses and caregivers. In addition, Hospice homes or care centers can provide 24-hour care to the dying like a nursing home, but with comfort-only as the constant focus.

After a loved one passes away, hospice service can continue to help family and friends through support groups, visits with a chaplain or social worker. Many people who have benefitted from Hospice in their families become Hospice volunteers to help guide others through the dying and grieving processes.

Hospice services can provide some financial relief for the elderly and their loved ones because Hospice services are covered by Medicare. You won't get a charge for Hospice services, and Hospice medications and supplies are not charged to the patient.

The biggest problem with Hospice isn't really Hospice's problem at all. The biggest problem is that Hospice is brought in very late in the dying process. People can be admitted to Hospice if they are expected to pass away in the next 6 months. Discussing and bringing in Hospice months or weeks before an expected death will help all of an elder's family reconcile with the fact that he is expected to die, and that no one is going to intervene or go through medical heroics to stop this. It decreases the stress and potential conflict in the last days of life if everyone has time to think about letting go.

If the senior you love is ready to just focus on comfort, and doesn't want interventions such as hospitalization or IVs, consider asking for a Hospice evaluation. You can do this by talking to a health care provider or contacting a local Hospice provider directly. Hospice providers can be affiliated with various health care organizations including hospital outreach programs, non-profit community-based groups, and for-profit home health agencies.

The final thing to consider about hospice is that people can always change their minds. A change of heart or a new medical breakthrough might make someone want to reconsider. Also, people do sometimes "graduate" from hospice if they get better or stabilize, and that is fine. Hospice can be brought back later if your loved one becomes ill again.

How Do We Pay for All of This?

In previous sections, I have mentioned various forms of insurance and payment for senior care. But I wanted to include a dedicated section to review this information. Like all insurances and government programs, paying for elder care is complicated. It may take time and repeated study to understand the mechanisms of possible options for payment. As a nurse in elder care, I always half-jokingly told families "I'm a nurse, they don't let me manage the money." That was partially true. I could not base my assessment of an elder's needs on what they could or wanted to pay. I had to complete an honest care assessment. So, I am dipping my toe into the financial part of care with as much hesitation as I dip my toe into mountain lakes in my home state of Idaho. I know this is a huge question for everyone and I am constantly surrounded by insurance, Medicare and Medicaid on a daily basis. But I'm not an expert on this. To be honest though, it gets very complicated, and I'm not sure anyone has a real handle on it.

The first part is getting "Medicare" and "Medicaid" straight. Medicare is for the elderly. Every citizen over 67 is eligible in the Unites States. There are now different Medicare plans though that cover different kinds of care – one covers hospital care, one covers medical equipment, one covers medications. It is very confusing, and I suggest you sit down with an advocate or insurance agent for guidance. The federal government sets rules about Medicare. You will hear people regularly mix up medicare and medicaid. Try this: medicare ends with an e – e for elderly.

Medicaid is for very low-income people in the United States. Medicaid covers all types of medical costs and to some extent depends on the state guidelines for qualification. States set rules about Medicaid eligibility and oversee the programs.

Are you ready for the next part? Elderly people can qualify for both Medicare and Medicaid. You just have to have the misfortune of being both elderly and poor. If you are Canadian or British or a citizen of some other country you can skip this whole confusing section.

Four main sources exist to pay for senior care: 1) personal finances; 2) Long-term care insurance; 3) Medicare and 4) Medicaid. Note! Long-term care insurance is not health insurance: it only pays for residential care. Medicare has a few variations at this time called Parts A, B, and C. Part A is available to help pay for skilled nursing and rehabilitation care. This is paid in full for a few weeks and then may pay part of the care for another few weeks. Please remember that these government and non-government insurances are always changing. We may see Medicare expand or contract over the next few years.

Having liquid personal assets for care is the easiest to understand. The elder or their loved ones pay costs out of pocket. At this time, expect $90,000 to $100,000 per year for skilled nursing; $50,000-$80,000 per year for assisted living or memory care, and $200,000-$250,000 per year for in-home 24-hour care. If your loved one has that kind of money, great, but I know that many people don't. It is especially difficult if you can expect a long time in need of care due to an illness such as Alzheimer's disease or Parkinson's disease.

Long-Term Care Insurance

Just like in any insurance package you may buy, long term care insurances vary greatly. Some older policies are indefinite. Most newer policies have more limited time frames such as two years of care. To qualify to use long term care insurance, an elder usually has to need help with three personal care tasks (ADLs) such as showering, toileting and transferring. Also, there is usually a self-pay period of one to three months before payment starts. Long-term care insurance usually reimburses the resident, they do not pay a care facility directly. Frequently, long-term care insurance providers will send their own nurse out to assess a resident to make sure they need the care being billed. These companies also require copies of bills and service agreements or care plans. Make a copy of anything you send to a long-term care company. In my experience, they are masters of losing documents, then denying claims. You cannot buy long-term care insurance later in life to cover costs of care. These are usually policies that an elder has paid on for decades. It is important to fight for these resources if they are available. As I understand it from insurance agents, insurance companies have found that these are a money loser for them, so they do not make it easy to claim the benefits.

Medicare

Currently, and for the past several decades medicare can pay for seniors and other people with long-term or permanent disability to get both medical services and skilled nursing facility care. In the US, there is a lot of discussion about expanding Medicare so remember, again, that this may change. Medicare covers the expenses of a short stay in a skilled nursing facility. If a resident qualifies, Medicare may pay fully for three weeks, then pay part of SNF costs for another nine weeks if therapy is needed and the resident is improving. They do not pay for assisted living, group homes or memory care. A senior has to qualify for medicare benefits to be deemed eligible for medicare payments to a nursing home. Usually, this qualification is a three-night stay after being admitted to a hospital. If you have had an experience with hospitals lately, you will know that you have to be very sick to stay for three nights.

After a qualifying hospital stay, a senior can go to a skilled nursing facility (SNF) and stay about 3-12 weeks if they are making progress towards rehabilitation, or they need treatments and medications only available in an inpatient setting. This might include for example IV antibiotics multiple times a day for a serious infection, wound care, or post-surgical rehabilitation and therapy. Most people are in skilled nursing for rehabilitation services. So, they have to work with nursing, physical therapy, occupational therapy and/or speech therapy and continue to improve to get approval to stay with Medicare payment. If a senior plateaus, they can be sent to a lower level of care such as assisted living or home. Or, the senior or their family may choose to pay out-of-pocket.

Work closely with the SNF's social worker to keep tabs on whether your loved one is making progress, and what the discharge plans might be. This is a dynamic process and you may feel surprised by what feels like a rather sudden discharge notice. Social workers or discharge planners have to work to get appropriate placement for their residents. If you have a loved one who is difficult to place due to a lack of funds, medical or cognitive issues, this may take weeks. If your loved one has simple care needs and can pay privately for assisted living or in-home care then placement should go quickly.

Let me reiterate that I am not an expert on the finances of elder care. Although I work with it daily and have worked with insurances in a variety of settings. It still feels a bit like a black box to me. In the references, you will find some resources for more information. You can find more information on these websites and look for Medicare, Medicaid and long-term care insurance directly.[xxiii][xxiv]

Caring for the Caregiver

So far, we have covered many of the problems and worries you might face in helping a senior navigate the issues associated with aging, elder care and some of the possible resources that might help meet those needs. In my years of experience working with both seniors and their loved ones dealing with the ins and outs of the later years, I have personally helped people work through all of these issues. Or at least, I certainly hope that I have helped. Knowledge is power and you have made it through a lot of different possible scenarios of the needs you could face with your loved one. Now it is time to talk about you. Being a caregiver is difficult work. Depending on your circumstances, it can be taxing emotionally, physically and financially. But I wouldn't be in the field I am if I didn't think that it can also be joyful, meaningful and rewarding. Many of you are giving back to someone who supported you earlier in your life. You might think back on your years as a baby, toddler or teenager and think "well, that could not have been easy for my parents, so I am doing what isn't so easy for me now." You may not feel like you owe the person anything, but you are doing what you think is right and necessary. Whatever your reasons, know that you are providing valuable help to an elder, and know that there is not one right way to do this.

Setting Limits

Can you do it all? I can't. I might want to think I can fit all my work, family commitments, health commitments, financial balancing, and volunteer work into my life, but I regularly fail at something. I really used to try to go all out for everyone. Then, I gave birth to my third child and adopted my fourth child in rapid succession giving me virtual twin girls. I think I volunteered for a couple of things after they arrived, but I always failed at keeping my commitments and had to back out. So, when they were young, it wasn't my time to volunteer in my community while they were little. No that's a lie, I am just starting to dip my toe into volunteering for things at their school and they just turned 13. It's been a long and busy road. I still set serious limits, and say I can do this one school field trip, or that one day of painting walls at the school but that is it. No committees or on-going jobs. I set limits. And you have to, too. My juggling act might be with my career, kids and health, and yours might be juggling marriage, job and helping your loved one, but the limit setting is the same. You are a less effective helper if you are burned out. So, do all those things clichés tell us: Put your own oxygen mask on before helping others; fill your own cup before filling others because you can't pour from an empty cup... We all know these things to be true. So, when you feel yourself not able to cope with helping your elder loved one, take some time for yourself and evaluate your limits.

Dividing Up Care

One of the best ways to manage the amount of help you are providing for your senior loved one is to divide and conquer the tasks at hand. To do this you have to ASK FOR HELP. Help, yes, ask for it. If one person does everything, then they are more at risk of burnout and frustration. That doesn't help anyone as times goes by. There are many ways to divide needs. The two basic ways are dividing by tasks and by time. Tasks can be divided by the skills of various loved ones – if a nephew is great at cooking, he can provide meals. If your niece has time in her schedule to take grandma to senior lunches, then she can add that to her schedule. If you choose to go with this model, try to make an extensive list of needs and encourage all the senior's friends and supporters to pick a task or two or three… Often, there are a lot of friends and supporters who want to help, but they often just aren't sure what to do.

Helping a senior can also be divided up by time in a variety of creative ways. Some families divide up help by days or weeks, others divided up by months. For example, for years, my aunt and her sisters and brother took care of their mother by having her visit them in their homes around the US. Her mother, whose real name was Katherine, but who we all called "Grandma Jack" because one of the many grandchildren and cousins couldn't say Katherine so somehow someone began calling her by the same name as her husband so we ended up with "Grandpa Jack" and "Grandma Jack." When Grandma Jack moved from home to home of her daughters' and son, they had the time and energy to enjoy her visits before she moved on to the next house. She got to visit everyone, not pay rent or for care, and she didn't get lonely separated from her children scattered across the US. Eventually, as she became less mobile, Grandma Jack stayed at one daughter's home and the other brother and sisters visited and helped.

Other families may divide up care by days of the week or pretty much any other time slot that can be thought up. A son may help his parent on Friday and Saturday, while a daughter takes Monday and Wednesday. Any combination works and you can also add in paid caregivers if needed.

Attachment and Responsibility

Some of us had beautiful, loving childhoods, and want to take care of our parents or other family members out of devotion, and a sense of wanting to give back all that was given to us. Some of us have negative feelings towards our elders or parents and are torn between feeling obligated, resentful and just wishing things were different. This is part of the reason that there is no one best model for caring for elders and especially parents. You may want to spend every moment with your loved one, or you may feel that you just want to make sure they are safe and not really be part of their lives. It is never too late to try to repair a relationship but know that you are not obligated to be a martyr again for an abusive or absent parent. Guilt isn't a very productive emotion. Just set your limit on what you feel comfortable doing and do that.

I have worked with several sons and daughters who are the only thing that their mothers or fathers have left. My residents have included fathers with dementia who have to be moved across the country to live near a son who has not seen him in 40 years. I have worked with mothers with mental illness who had to be rescued from exploitive situations in her elder years, only to resentfully accept help from an estranged daughter.

Difficult relationships make the challenges of cognitive decline even more difficult. It's easy to feel like your parent with dementia is trying to drive you crazy, or to push your buttons. If this is your situation, work with professional healthcare workers to carry as much of the load as possible. Do what you think is right or what you feel you can endure. Set a goal for visits and interaction such as "I'm going to take mom to the grocery for a half hour then get her settled back in her apartment, then I'm going home." Or, I will attend Dad's care conferences and make sure he is getting the care he needs, but I am not going to spend large amounts of time with him. Sometimes professional staff can work really well with your estranged elders. When working with people who have difficult relationships with their elders, they have often told me or the caregivers I work with "I don't know how you deal with her!" and I tell them "because she can't push my buttons like she can yours." So, I strongly encourage you to set limits if you have past or current conflict with a senior loved one, make your feelings known if you think it will be productive, and hire professional care to help as much as you can.

Facing Loss

Elder care is full of joy, and full of loss. Mostly seniors experience slow and steady loss in their later years. Declines in senses, declines in mobility and declines in cognition are slow processes, but they are mourned just the same. Both the senior and their loved ones tend to mourn these losses. Still, facing a final loss of a loved one can seem like it comes too quickly. As much as we might know that our friend is 90 and in failing health, dealing with the final weeks, days and inevitable death can seem like it sneaks up on you. No matter how prepared you feel, the end can still be difficult. The more prepared everyone is and the more clarity you have regarding your loved ones wishes, the easier this will be. Here are some sample questions you can review with your loved one. These are also at the end of the book as a worksheet, and available to print from my website www.juliaparkerconsulting.com.

End-of-Life Wishes

Encourage your elderly loved one to complete these statements for himself or herself. You can also do these for yourself or as a guide for what you would want for your loved one, and for other caregivers who will face the end-of-life stages with you and your loved one.

- I believe when people die…
- I have valued these things in life…
- I really don't care about these things that other people seem to…
- I want to be let go or let to die if…

- I believe I will be more afraid at the end of life if…
- I believe I will feel more comfort at the end of life if…
- I think the best possible death would look like this…
- Please do these things at the end of my life…
- Please don't do these things at the end of my life…
- If I can't say my final goodbyes, I want my loved ones to know…

Because people often tell me that they didn't know what to expect or ask me what to expect, I want to share with you the very typical death I have seen in elder care. Death that occurs when someone is being assisted by Hospice or under some other palliative care looks like this most of the time. For the aged, death is usually a gentle process. There are not a lot of dramatics. No last words followed by a flat-line on the heart rate monitor. People slip away over a few days until they no longer have enough consciousness to speak or interact. Breathing slows and becomes irregular for the last day or hours. The heart has less ability to pump blood to the extremities so the skin of the fingers and toes becomes dusky blue or gray. Longer and longer gaps occur between breaths. A dying person may breathe 3 times in rapid succession then have a 30 second gap. Then there is usually a last deep breath and sigh. The heart stops. A nurse or doctor will listen for heart tones and absent those will declare death. These planned and expected deaths will be followed by a visit from the Hospice nurse if he or she isn't already there and then you can say goodbyes while the funeral home prepares to come. Funeral home employees will remove the body when you are ready.

At this point, families are probably still experiencing a lot of disbelief and adrenaline. The next days are usually filled with calls and visits from family and friends, projects, moving and preparation. Perhaps a memorial service – although many people are holding off on those until extended family can plan a trip and gather. However, this is also a good time to look into support groups and services. Hospitals and Hospice can give you referrals to support services.

If you were a caregiver of someone you lost, it leaves a hole in your life. Both a real hole in your schedule where time used to be filled with tasks, and an emotional hole of losing someone you loved. Take a little time to try out a support group. Sharing experiences and a few kind words with others can ease the grief. It definitely won't hurt to try it.

Concluding Thoughts

I started this book by saying thank you and I want to say it again. Navigating elder care is a lot of work. It can be emotionally, physically and financially challenging. You are doing this out of love. It may be perfect, wonderful, healthy, well-reciprocated love between a parent and a child, or it may be a gritty, family-is-family, difficult, take-care-of your-own kind of love.

Take these thoughts with you on your journey:

- You are helping someone who is vulnerable and in need.
- You can set limits to do what you can and also take care of yourself.
- There is no one right way to help an elder loved one.
- Ask for help; from other friends and families, from healthcare providers, from professional caregivers and from anyone else available. Then, accept that help.
- Make room for moments of connection and joy with your elder loved one.

It is my greatest hope that this book helps you along the journey of navigating elder care. This field, this career I have had has brought me so much meaning and joy. My favorite parts of my professional life have been helping families and loved ones help elders, and in the moments of joy and meaning that can be found along the difficult road of navigating elder care. I hope that you can find those moments of joy and meaning along your road.

Medication Management

Name:

Date of Birth:

Medication Name	Dose	Frequency	Reason	Side Effects/Concerns	Prescriber

Date Last Reviewed:

Name/Title of Reviewer:

Vitamins, Herbs and Other Supplements

Name:

Date of Birth:

Supplement/Vitamin	Dose	Frequency	Reason	Side Effects/Concerns

Date Last Reviewed:

Name/Title of Reviewer:

Non-prescription or over-the-counter medication

Name:

Date of Birth:

Over-the-counter	Dose	Frequency	Reason	Side Effects/ Concerns

Date Last Reviewed:

Name/Title of Reviewer:

Creams, lotions, eyedrops, ear drops, nose spray

Name:
Date of Birth:

Medication	Dose	Frequency	Reason	Side Effects/ Concerns

Date Last Reviewed:
Name/Title of Reviewer:

Basic Personal Care Needs

Type of Care	On my own	Need limited assistance – describe	Need full assistance – describe
Bathing or Showering			
Shampooing			
Toileting			
Dressing			
Transferring			
Ambulation/Walking			
Feeding			
Hair brushing			
Teeth brushing			
Shaving			
Toenails			
Fingernails			

Type of Care	Who will help	Schedule	Contact information
Bathing or Showering			
Shampooing			
Toileting			
Dressing			
Transferring			
Ambulation/ Walking			
Feeding			
Hair brushing			
Teeth brushing			
Shaving			
Toenails			
Fingernails			

Complex Care Needs

Type of Care	On my own	Need limited assistance – describe	Need full assistance – describe
Laundry			
Cooking			
Banking			
Bill Paying			
House cleaning			
Lawn/garden			
Transportation			
Health care appointments			
Socializing			
Exercising			
Managing medications			
Technology – phone, internet, cable, TV			

Laundry			
Cooking			
Banking			
Bill Paying			
House cleaning			
Lawn/garden			
Transportation			
Health care appointments			
Socializing			
Exercising			
Managing medications			
Technology – phone, internet, cable, TV			

Doctor or Health Care Provider Appointment Organizations

Name:

Date of Birth:

Appointment time:

Length of time scheduled:

Purpose of appointment:

Questions for provider: (Up to 3 for 15-minute appointment. Up to 5 for 30-minute appointment)

1.

2.

3.

4.

5.

Provider thoughts on questions/concerns:

1.

2.

3.

4.

5.

New medication prescriptions:

New lifestyle/care recommendations:

Labs scheduled:

Therapy scheduled:

New appointments or referrals:

Emergency Room/Ambulance Information

Name:

Date of Birth:

Normal cognitive status:

I usually understand:

___ my name

___ my age

___ the date

___ the time of day

___ where I am

___ what is happening around me

For help, I rely on these people:

Normally I can:

___ walk

___ talk

___ feed myself

___ stand on my own

___ go to the bathroom on my own

I need these assistive devices:

___ hearing aids

___ glasses

___ walker

___ cane

___ wheelchair

Primary health care provider:

Specialists:

Code status:

Pharmacy:

Allergies:

Questions for Facilities – Care Provided	
Questions	**Facility Answers**
What care do you provide?	
How do residents request help?	
What is the average wait for a call light during each shift?	
What kinds of behaviors are you used to dealing with in residents with dementia?	
Can you provide transportation?	
Can I see an activity calendar?	
Can I see a monthly menu?	
Can you accommodate special diets?	
Can residents eat meals in their rooms? Does it cost more?	

Questions for Facilities – Cost Calculations	
Question	**Facility Answers**
How do you calculate care costs?	
Is the cost for care in addition to the rent for the room?	
Can I have the preliminary care costs before we move in?	
Do they take any insurance?	
What happens if we run out of money and have to use Medicaid?	

Questions for Facilities – Outside Services	
Question	**Facility Answers**
Do you use a specific pharmacy?	
Do I have to use your pharmacy? Is there an extra charge if we don't?	
If applicable, can we use VA?	
Do you have a health care provider who comes in to see residents?	
Do you have physical therapy, occupational therapy or speech therapy?	
Do you work with an outside Hospice provider?	

Questions for Facilities – Environment and Facility

Question	Facility Answers
Can I see your last state survey?	
Is this a locked facility?	
Is there an outside area to walk safely?	
Do residents have their own bathrooms?	
Do residents have their own showers?	
Can residents keep their doors open?	
Can residents adjust the heat in their own rooms?	
Will my loved one have to share a room or apartment?	

Questions for Facilities: Staffing	
Questions	**Facility Answers**
Do you have licensed nurses in the building? How many hours/day?	
What kind of training do your care staff get?	
What is your care staff to resident ratio?	
What is your care staff to resident ratio for each shift?	
How many hours per day do staff work?	
What do you pay your care staff?	
What is your turnover rate for staff?	

End-of-Life Wishes

Consider your final weeks and days on Earth. What do you want to happen during that time? These final wishes are a gift to your loved ones. A last communication of the warmth and love between you, and a way to ease both your and their transitions. I believe when people die…

I have valued these things in life…
I really don't care about these things that other people seem to…
I want to be let go or let to die if…

I believe I will be more afraid at the end of life if…

I believe I will feel more comfort at the end of life if…

I think the best possible death would look like this…

Please don't do these things at the end of my life…

Please do these things at the end of my life…

If I can't say my final goodbyes, I want my loved ones to know…

Endnotes

[i] National Council of Certified Dementia Practitioners. 2020. www.nccdp.org

[ii] Guo, H. and Sapra, A. 2020. Instrumental Activity of Daily Living (IADL) https://www.ncbi.nlm.nih.gov/books/NBK553126/

[iii] Sanders, L. 2019. LeadingAge NORC Poll: Older Baby Boomers' Preferences on Aging. March 18, 2019 https://www.leadingage.org/press-release/leadingage-norc-poll-older-baby-boomers-preferences-aging

[iv] Anderson, A. and Loeser, R. 2010. Why is Osteoarthritis An Age-Related Disease? Best Practice Clinical Rheumatology. 2010. Feb: 24 (1) https://www.ncbi.nlm.nih.gov/pmc/articles/PMC2818253/

[v] Fit and Fall Proof 2020. http://idahopublichealth.com/community/fitandfallproof

[vi] Stay Active and Independent for Life. 2020. https://docs.wistatic.com/ugd/da1f4d_69e18148549845f9b06de5b17a62f2ca.pdf

[vii] Alzheimer's Disease Facts and Figures. 2018. www.alz.org/media/documents/facts-and-figures-2018-r.pdf

[viii] Zeisel, J. 2009. I'm Still Here. A New Philosophy of Alzheimer's Care. Avery Publishing.

[ix] Doidge, N. 2015. The Brain's Way of Healthing: Remarkable Discoveries and Recoveries from The Frontiers of Neuroplasticity. Penguin.

[x] National Institute on Aging. 2020. Parkinson's Disease. https://www.nia.nih.gov/health/what-lewy-body-dementia

[xi] National Institute on Aging. 2020. What is Lewy Body Dementia? https://www.nia.nih.gov/health/what-lewy-body-dementia.

[xii] Chayer, C and M. Freedman. Current Neurology Neuroscience Report. 2001 November 1 (6) 547-552

[xiii] Washington Post 2017/12/08

[xiv] American Association of Retired Persons. 2020. Fraud Watch Network. www.aarp.org/money/scams-fraud/

[xv] National Council on Aging. 2020. www.ncoa.org/economic-security/money-management/scams-security/top-10-scams-targeting-seniors/

[xvi] https://questions-seniordriving.aaa.com/conversations-with-family/reporting-unsafe-driver-2/

[xvii] National Council on Aging. 2020. NCOA, org/public-policy-action/elder-justice/elder abuse facts//3intrapagenov2

[xviii] Elder Justice Act. 2006. https://www.congress.gov/bill/111th-congress/house-bill/2006/text?format=txt

[xix] National POLST. 2020. https://polst.org

[xx] Medicare Basics. 2020. https://www.cms.gov/Outreach-and-Education/Medicare-Learning-Network-MLN/MLN-Products/Acronyms/Acronyms-908999.html

[xxi] Facts about Women and Alzheimer's 2020. http://www.alz.org/raiseyourvoice/overview.asp

[xxii] U.S. Department of Veterans Administration. 2020. www.va.gov/find-locations/

[xxiii] American Association of Retired Persons. Health Tool. Undesrstanding Medicare. 2020. https://www.aarp.org/health/medicare-qa-tool/understanding-medicare/

[xxiv]Medicaid.gov 2020 Contact Your State.
https://www.medicaid.gov/about-us/contact-us/contact-your-state-questions/index.html